# Heart of a Warrior

7 Ancient
Secrets
to a
Great Life

Jim Langlas

free spirit
PUBLISHING®

**Library of Congress Cataloging-in-Publication Data**
Langlas, Jim.
  Heart of a warrior : 7 ancient secrets to a great life / by Jim Langlas.
    p. cm.
  Includes index.
  ISBN 978-1-57542-388-3
  1. Self-control. 2. Virtues. 3. Discipline. 4. Leadership.  I. Title.
  BF632.L325 2011
  170'.44—dc23

2011038176

eBook ISBN: 978-1-57542-672-3

*Note:* The names of the teens quoted in this book have been changed to protect their privacy.

Reading Level Grades 5–6; Interest Level Ages 12 & up;
Fountas & Pinnell Guided Reading Level W

Edited by Alison Behnke
Cover and interior design by Michelle Lee

All illustrations by Michelle Lee, except circle illustration © copyright istockphoto/andylin. Thanks to Araleva for some of the brushes.

10 9 8 7 6 5 4 3 2 1
Printed in the United States of America
S18860212

**Free Spirit Publishing Inc.**
Minneapolis, MN
(612) 338-2068
help4kids@freespirit.com
www.freespirit.com

**Printed on recycled paper**

including 50% post-consumer waste

Free Spirit Publishing is a member of the Green Press Initiative, and we're committed to printing our books on recycled paper containing a minimum of 30% post-consumer waste (PCW). For every ton of books printed on 30% PCW recycled paper, we save 5.1 trees, 2,100 gallons of water, 114 gallons of oil, 18 pounds of air pollution, 1,230 kilowatt hours of energy, and .9 cubic yards of landfill space. At Free Spirit it's our goal to nurture not only young people, but nature too!

**green press** INITIATIVE

In gratitude and love, *Heart of a Warrior* is dedicated to my wife Michelle, my son Jack, and my daughter Chelsea.

# Contents

# Introduction

## Entering the World of the Warrior

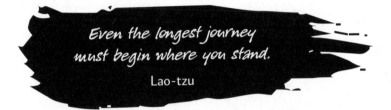

> *Even the longest journey must begin where you stand.*
>
> Lao-tzu

You are about to enter the world of the warrior. Once you enter it, you will discover that it is a world of action, and that this action is rooted in belief and character. It is a noble and an honorable world. The modern warrior—whom you may choose to become—does not want to fight others. Instead, the warrior strives to conquer the self, and to live with power and peace, confidence and joy, even in difficult times. The true warrior's spirit can never be defeated.

The roots of warrior culture stretch far back in time. Throughout history and all around the world, the warrior has been a powerful symbol—a symbol of strength and courage, and also of integrity and creativity. Over the centuries, many different groups of warriors have earned the respect and gratitude of their people. The warrior tradition includes the European knights of the Middle Ages, the Japanese samurai, and the Spartans of ancient Greece.

One unique group of warriors lived in Asia nearly 1,500 years ago. In the ancient kingdom of Silla, located on the Korean Peninsula, a band of warriors strived to protect their

1

small homeland from the attacks of much larger neighboring kingdoms. These warriors were called the Hwarangdo (pronounced hwah-rahng-DOE), meaning "Flower Knights." This group included many courageous teenagers, as well as older warriors who guided them. Some historians think that the original leaders of the Hwarangdo were two women appointed by King Jinheung of Silla. These female leaders, known as Won Hwa ("Original Flower"), focused not on honing battle skills, but on the cultural development of the young Hwarangdo.

The Hwarangdo trained in the martial arts, swordsmanship, and horseback riding. They conditioned their bodies by swimming in cold rivers during the wintertime and climbing mountains in the heat of the summer. They strengthened their spirits by playing music, dancing, and writing poetry. When they grew into adults, they became leaders of their towns and of their kingdom.

The Hwarangdo were a powerful force, and they lived according to a disciplined code of honor. Here are the five basic elements of this ancient code:

- Be loyal to your king.
- Love and respect your parents and elders.
- Be honorable and trustworthy with your friends.
- Never retreat in battle.
- Use careful judgment when confronting your enemy.

The code of the Hwarangdo eventually formed the foundation of the five modern principles of the Korean martial art of Taekwondo. These principles are:

- Courtesy
- Integrity
- Perseverance
- Self-control
- Indomitable spirit

Centuries later, Master Cha Kyo Han, founder of the Universal Taekwondo Federation, added two more principles. These principles, which show character in action, are:

- Community service
- Love

*Heart of a Warrior* will take you into the inner circle of a group of young warriors similar to the Hwarangdo. They are studying the warrior's path, learning from their wise, elderly teacher. In each chapter, the master explores one of the seven principles with his students. Each of these principles, in turn, consists of four fundamentals that focus on specific parts of the bigger picture.

You'll find tales in this book about ancient warriors. You'll also find stories about modern warriors, teenagers like you. The sections called "Voice of a Warrior" and "A Story from the Warrior's Path" feature writings directly from those teens, recounting how they've put the ideas in *Heart of a Warrior* into action in their own lives. All of these stories can serve as personal guides for you as you practice the way of the warrior. Be on the lookout for the "Room for Reflection" sections, too. Each one poses questions that you can think about, talk about, or write about as you strengthen your warrior's heart.

My own background is in Taekwondo. I've studied this art since I was a teenager, and I also taught it for many years. So the seven principles in this book are closely tied to the practice of that specific field. Many other martial arts draw upon similar principles. So do a variety of philosophies and belief systems from Korea, other East Asian countries, and cultures all over the world. You might already be familiar with similar ideas and character traits from school or elsewhere.

You do not have to train in the martial arts or study ancient philosophies to be a modern warrior. All of us have room in our lives for these simple but powerful ideas. The world is full of happy, productive people who live by these principles every day. Modern warriors are all around us. They achieve joy, build meaningful relationships with others, gain success, and help create a more peaceful world. With determination, guidance, and practice, you can be one of them.

Being a warrior is not always easy, and embracing the principles in this book doesn't mean that you won't sometimes feel angry, resentful, sad, or lonely. We all have these emotions. They are part of life, and they are part of the warrior's path. You don't need to stifle your feelings—or hide your true self and your own unique character—to succeed as a warrior. Rather, by thinking about these ideas and doing your best to live by them, even when it's difficult, you will discover how much courage and strength you already have within you. You *already* have the heart of a warrior.

As you begin and continue your journey, you might wish to share a few of your thoughts and experiences. You may have interesting and revealing stories or insights that will encourage other warriors. Please feel free to share them with me by emailing me at help4kids@freespirit.com, visiting my website at www.jameslanglas.com, or sending them to me in care of the following address:

Free Spirit Publishing
217 Fifth Avenue North, Suite 200
Minneapolis, MN 55401-1299

Best wishes to you,

*Jim Langlas*

If you keep a green bough in your heart, the singing bird will come.

Chinese proverb

# The First Principle
# *Courtesy*

The little clearing in the grove where the class met each day was empty when the students arrived that morning. The leaves of the birch trees rustled in the springtime breeze, and the grass was soft and green. Just beyond the trees rippled a stream carrying the fresh, cold water of melted snow, with which the students brewed their tea each dawn and washed their faces each night. Above them, sparrows and wrens chattered as they flitted from branch to branch.

It was peaceful here among the birch trees—peaceful, beautiful, and safe. But the student-warriors knew very well that not all the world was so serene. Beyond their idyllic classroom lay a world often torn by greed, jealousy, anger, and war. It was because of this strife that they were here now, preparing themselves for lives of action, lives of noble deeds both large and small. With their teacher, Master Yi, they studied the principles of an ancient art and an ancient path—the path of the warrior.

As they waited for their teacher, two students practiced their sparring skills together. A third recited her poetry and a fourth sketched the pleasant scene before him. Others simply sat on the sun-dappled grass and meditated, breathing slowly and deeply.

Finally, their teacher appeared. His flowing robe was the same as always; his long white beard as gleaming as ever. But

1

something seemed different. In his brow was a new wrinkle—wasn't there? Or was there, perhaps, a touch more silver in his beard? Each student glanced around at the others in the group, wondering if they too sensed a change.

The master smiled at his students, whom he had come to know well in the recent months. He cleared his throat and said softly, "In one week, I will leave you."

The glances among the students now grew swifter, more urgent. Leave? So soon?

Before they could protest or question, Master Yi went on, his voice quiet but very firm. There was no room in his tone for argument.

"It is best that I do leave you. The greatest learning often takes place after the teacher has left. I have taught you, and I have asked you to practice. In my absence, you must determine for yourselves how much you have learned—and how well.

"Before I go, I have seven lessons to share with you. Remember that my words will never substitute for your living. Always make words real by your actions.

"Let us begin. Come, gather around me. Sit, and listen.

"Today we consider the principle of courtesy," Master Yi told his students. "First, honor all things and all beings in your heart. Recognize that you are greater than no other. When you see yourself connected to the world and to others, you will know respect. The depth of your feeling will show itself through the depth of your action.

"Greet the world with a soft palm, not with a fist. Bow low to your neighbor. The sound of one unkind word from your lips will echo in your ears and return to the source: your own heart."

The teacher looked around the grove, studying the faces of his pupils to see if they understood him.

"Your souls already carry the seeds of courtesy and deep respect," he continued. "We all wish for these things, after all. But when you show courtesy, do not say, 'I will do this so that I may receive courtesy in return.' Too often we worry about receiving it rather than giving it. When we begin to seek something, we cannot know where we should look for it. And the more we try to seize something for ourselves by force, the more elusive it becomes. Instead, you must give freely and openly. Only then will the seeds grow: when you water them with compassion and nurture them with soft hands."

At this, one of the students scoffed—though he did not allow the master to hear him. He stood up, tall and proud, and asked, "What do soft hands have to do with us? We are warriors. We toughen our hands and our feet to make them into great weapons."

The master replied, "Weapons to fight against whom? Before you do battle, you must always remember that the greatest enemy is within yourself. You cannot use a sword to fight the enemy inside your own heart. But if you learn respect, you may one day make this enemy your ally and your friend."

Some of the students appeared puzzled. Master Yi continued, "Think hard. You must know that a respectful heart is a peaceful heart. If the heart is not at war with itself, why would it want to fight others? If you are kind to yourself, you will be kind to others, and if you are kind to others, you will be kind to yourself."

One student asked, "But what is the great enemy within ourselves?"

"Fear," replied Master Yi. "Fear is born of ignorance. So is cruelty. The true warrior is never cruel. He or she is kind—and secure in inner strength. Remember that all people are your brothers and your sisters, and you will never be ignorant. Then you will never be afraid, the enemy will fade away, and you will begin to share your knowledge with others."

The old teacher paused and said slowly, "If you demand kindness from others, you will not hear the music. Give kindness and you sing the song. The ice in yourself must thaw before you can drink the cool water."

Another student-warrior rose. She asked, "What is the difference between courtesy and respect?"

The teacher answered, "Respect is the root. Courtesy is the tree. Let your courtesy grow out of respect, and let these two ideals harmoniously guide your spirit. What is on the surface must reflect what is within."

Master Yi pondered deeply for a few moments. Finally he continued, "Touch the flower lightly. Do not crush its stem. While you may seem to be courteous in action, the body that acts without the heart's warmth caresses with a cold hand."

Master Yi motioned for his students to stand. Then he said:

Looking is good. Seeing is better. Listening is good. Hearing is better. Hear this poem with your hearts:

Looking over the side of this old boat,
I see my image in the blue-green deep.
This quiet water holds
my silent words,
my tender strength.

I can see the depths through the shallows,
as I rise to greet the world.

Dipping my palm
into the slippery coolness,
I know the truth at last.

I bow my head,
respecting my breath,
and your breath,
and row toward the trees,

toward the branches
that will shelter us all.

The students waited, watching Master Yi closely to be certain that he was finished with his lesson. When they saw him give a slight nod, they bowed to their teacher and filed silently out of the clearing.

# Four Fundamentals for the Warrior

On the first day of Master Yi's final week with his students, he focuses on the principle of courtesy. He reminds the young warriors that showing courtesy is a positive, powerful way to interact with others and with the world. The heart of a warrior is a respectful heart, which shows itself outwardly through courteous actions toward everyone.

The master also tells his pupils to give courtesy freely, not just so they may receive it in return. True warriors respect others and the world. They realize that their generous acts of courtesy come from a place of strength, not weakness. Master Yi makes it clear that the enemies of courtesy are fear and cruelty, because these so often arise when people do not recognize our common humanity.

To develop this first quality of a warrior, practice these four fundamentals:

- Be generous and genuine with your respect.
- Do not be afraid of rejection.
- Show courtesy toward all—even your rivals.
- See yourself in others.

## Be Generous and Genuine with Your Respect

*One day a group of warriors traveled through a small village on the way to see their country's king. They paused along the road to eat and rest, stopping near the home of a woman and her teenage son. The boy had heard many stories about his country's great warriors, and he longed to join them one day. He approached the oldest warrior and said, "Sir, I have dreamed of becoming a warrior. I think I am ready to begin my training. Will you take me along with you, so that I may join the ranks of these great warriors? Most of them are not much older than I am. I believe that I, too, could become a brave and noble warrior."*

*The older man looked at the boy carefully. "Where are your parents?" he asked. The boy replied, "My father is dead. My mother is inside, cleaning the house."*

*"Please ask her to come outside," said the warrior. The boy hurried into the house and soon reappeared, followed by a thin, limping woman. The warrior said to the boy, "Ask her if she will give you permission to begin your training with us." The son eagerly turned to his mother and asked her, but she grew quiet and sad, telling her son that she hoped he would stay with her a while longer. Seeing that his dream might not come true—at least not today—the boy grew very angry. He spoke harshly to his mother, and turned roughly away from her.*

*The warrior observed all this in silence. Finally he said to the boy, "I can see that you truly wish to join us, but your actions have shown me that you are not yet ready. Your mother gave you life. She cares for you. Yet you show no courtesy toward her. You have not received her affection warmly, and you do not give her your gratitude. Nor do you try to understand her position. She loves you with her whole heart and does not want to lose you—yet you are thinking only of yourself."*

*The warrior continued, "You showed me courtesy by calling me 'sir,' but your courtesy does not run deep. You have shown no kindness to your mother. Go and let true respect take root in your heart. That is the first step on the path to becoming a warrior."*

Just as the boy in this story was unkind to his mother, we all fail to be respectful and courteous now and then. Sometimes it's especially hard to remember to show respect to the people we know best, and those we're closest to. Think about it: how often have you found yourself arguing loudly with your dad or mom, yelling at your little brother, or saying mean things to your best friend? Maybe you simply take these people for granted sometimes. You might lash out at them when you're angry or sad—just because they happen to be around you. Or, because you care about them so deeply, you may find that you get very sad or very angry with them if they hurt your feelings, even if they don't do so on purpose. But precisely because these people are so important to us, it's extra important that we try to be respectful to them. Our relationships with them are among our most valuable possessions, and we need to protect these relationships.

Now, when it comes to strangers, you might think that it sounds foolish to just hand them your respect without even getting to know them. Some people believe that others must earn our respect. It's true that lasting respect is often built on trust and friendship. And when people hurt us, make poor choices, or treat us or others badly, it can sometimes lessen our respect for them. But *everyone* deserves a basic amount of respect because, as Master Yi says, we are all "brothers and sisters." We share a common humanity. We all have faults—and we all have value. Knowing this also allows us to accept the respect of others. You have the right to be respected and valued for who you are. And chances are, if you're a person who is generous with your respect for others, they'll be more likely to respect you in return.

Living according to this fundamental isn't easy all the time, or in every situation. But if you can remember that everyone you meet appreciates being treated with courtesy and deserves to be respected as a human being, then you will begin to practice the principle of courtesy. Part of your growth as a warrior centers on being aware of *why* we act the way we do and on thinking about how *you* want to be treated. Depending on the situation, you can ask yourself some questions before you act: Is now the time for a kind word? Is it best that I not say anything? Could that person be rude because someone has hurt her? What can I do or say to make my friend feel more comfortable?

A warrior takes deliberate action—and with small but careful action, you can start building this principle little by little, day by day. The opportunities for small but powerful acts of courtesy are almost limitless: You might motion to a classmate to enter the classroom before you. You can greet your parents with a friendly smile. You could ask your sister how her biology class is going.

Warriors think of others before they think of themselves. They show respect and extend courtesy freely. And in doing so, they give a part of themselves to everyone they meet and everyone they know.

**Voice of a Warrior**

*"Once I started being courteous to others, others began being courteous to me."*

—Hector, 14

## Do Not Be Afraid of Rejection

All people want to be loved and respected. Naturally, we feel better when others say kind words to us and treat us well. It's certainly a lot easier to be nice to others when they are nice to you. Perhaps you've realized that some people's harsh words or negative attitudes come from their feelings of being rejected, lonely, or unloved. But what will you do when you are treated poorly? How would you feel and react if a stranger or acquaintance were rude to you for no reason? Or what if someone you thought was your friend suddenly stopped talking to you, or spread nasty rumors about you?

There's no doubt about it—this is tough stuff to deal with. Being kind can be a big risk sometimes. Other people won't always receive your kindness graciously. And when you've made yourself vulnerable by offering your friendship, your kindness, or your respect, rejection can hurt a lot. These are the moments to call upon the power, the awareness, and the resilience of the warrior. The pain that you feel will be real, but you may find that you can gradually release it by continuing to practice courtesy.

Your courtesy is rooted in your knowledge and understanding that all people share common needs and desires, and that we all are weak and vulnerable at times. This knowledge cannot be taken away from you. When you run into someone who hurts you or is mean to you, this knowledge gives you the power to give kindness where it may not be "deserved." The warrior understands that courtesy is not necessarily "deserved." It is given with no thought of receiving anything in return. Even if someone says an unkind word to you, that person does not take away your knowledge or your power to act positively.

One of the best ways to nurture your courtesy is to prepare yourself to take a small risk—and then take it! Prepare yourself for the possibility of rejection or an unkind word, and then seek the challenge of being kind. Try saying hello to someone you don't know. Or calmly tell the impolite store clerk that you appreciate his service and you hope he has a nice day. You might even attempt to patch up a broken relationship by telling a former friend that you'd like to go to a movie together, just as you used to do.

Taking a risk with courtesy has the potential to bring you rich rewards. Besides strengthening yourself as a warrior, you might regain an old friend or make a new one.

Continuing to offer kindness to others—even knowing you may be rejected—is always a positive action. And you might not even see all of the benefits right away. Who knows? Perhaps your courtesy will inspire courtesy in someone else.

## Show Courtesy Toward All— Even Your Rivals

You may know that the act of bowing in some cultures and in the martial arts is a sign of courtesy and respect. Some historians think that the tradition of bowing goes back many centuries, when opponents bowed to offer each other their heads, extending their necks toward the swords of their adversaries. In a way, this act—rooted in honor—is the ultimate sign of respect and trust. Each warrior trusted that the other would not chop off his head without first engaging in fair and honorable combat. This tradition is still alive in some modern practices of the martial arts. For example, when Taekwondo teachers show their students how to bow, they tell them to look at the ground as a sign of the greatest respect. If the students look into the eyes of the other, they are showing that they lack complete trust in their opponents.

Just because you don't fight off your enemies with a sword doesn't meant that courtesy among rivals isn't part of

### Room for Reflection

- How is courtesy related to courage?
- What do you think Master Yi means when he says, "Respect is the root. Courtesy is the tree"?
- How does our world encourage—and discourage—courtesy?
- Whom would you like to treat more courteously? Think about your relationship with this person and why you may not be as courteous as you could be. How could you show more courtesy to him or her?
- In your experience, is it possible to be both gentle and strong? How can these two qualities exist together?

your life. As you build your warrior's heart, you may be able to show courtesy even in difficult situations. You've probably met people who don't seem to have a lot of respect for anyone or anything. For example, if you play a sport, you may have faced someone who "trash talks"—swearing at you and hurling insults. Or perhaps you've been the target of harsh words in a classroom or lunchroom. Someone may have said to you, "You're not smart enough to be part of our project," or "We don't want *you* to sit with us. This is *our* lunch table."

Situations like these are hard to handle. You might be tempted to respond with angry words of your own. But even when faced with this kind of challenge—and temptation—the warrior can be courteous and noble. How? By remembering that such comments are usually a result of human weakness. Sometimes people try to elevate themselves by putting others below them. Their derogatory remarks are intended to make you feel inferior. This is the time to show your warrior's heart.

If you are faced with ridicule or harsh words, you may try to ignore them. But perhaps you can think of ways to respond in a strong and honorable way. After being insulted in an athletic competition, you might encourage your teammates to seek out the opposing players and shake hands with each of them. You might approach their coach before or after a contest and say, "We appreciate the challenge of facing your team today."

Silence can also be powerful. If you're rejected or insulted by a group of students, smiling and walking away can show not only strength but also commitment to a warrior spirit. With practice and determination, warriors can even come to view challenges to their courtesy as opportunities that will, ultimately, help them grow. Have you ever acted courteously when others around you did not? How did you feel? How did others react?

Think about a high school volleyball team that makes it to the state playoffs for the first time in its school's history. In the first round, the newcomer will face a team with a long record of success at the state tournament. On the morning of the game, a local newspaper features pictures of the star players from each team. A quotation beneath the picture of the player from the team with a winning history reads, "We really expect to make it to the finals." Beneath the picture of the star player from the newest team ran this statement: "We will make her eat those words."

There's a big difference between the words of these two players. The first player is full of optimism. She is focused on her team's performance. The second player, on the other hand, is more confrontational. Maybe she thinks that tough talk will make her team tough. Or she might worry that, because her team is new to the tournament, they need to act aggressively to earn respect. What do you think you would have said if you were interviewed in a similar situation?

Those with a warrior's heart show the opposition that while the matchup may be a "battle"—and while each team genuinely wants to win—the game is also a chance to show courtesy. A warrior's response might go something like this: "We know that our opponents are skilled and worthy, but we're confident that our team will demonstrate our talent and character and bring home the trophy."

Or maybe you have always prided yourself in your ability to do well in a particular subject in school, and you find yourself competing with a classmate for the highest grade in that class. Competition can often bring out the best in people, but it's also pretty easy to respond to such a situation with suspicion and mistrust. Maybe you'd be tempted to isolate yourself from the other student, even if you're friends. You might find yourself feeling angry when he or she does well on a quiz, or you might even try to distract or sabotage your rival. But what would a warrior do? Could a warrior find ways to help everyone grow and improve? Could a warrior find an opportunity to encourage and inspire others? Perhaps he or she would offer to study with the other successful student, knowing that both pupils have things to teach each other. What would you do?

Remember what Master Yi said to his young warriors: "Greet the world with a soft palm, not with a fist."

**Voice of a Warrior**

"When I started Taekwondo, I learned what courtesy really meant. Courtesy could be shown not just in the dojang at the Taekwondo studio, but with family and friends. A door held open, chores done for a neighbor—signs of courtesy. Acts of kindness and respect."

—Isabel, 15

## See Yourself in Others

*In an ancient kingdom, a terrible famine swept across the land. People in every village were starving. Even after thousands of people had perished, there seemed to be no relief in sight. The king called together the generals of his army, as well as his best and most noble warriors. When he asked them what they thought he should do to relieve the suffering, there was a long discussion, but no resolution. Finally, one warrior—a boy of about 17—asked to speak. He stood and bowed to his king before saying calmly, "I realize that what I am going to say might not be very popular. Nevertheless, I feel that I must say it. Because we are your warriors, you make sure that we are well fed, even as others in your kingdom starve. Certainly you want us to be strong so that we can defend the land from any outside threat. But our greatest enemy—starvation—is now in our midst, and it is killing your people—the very people we serve to defend. I propose that you reduce the amount of food that you set aside for the warriors. Then we can take the extra supplies to our villages to feed the people."*

*The king nodded. "The kingdom is in grave danger. This may truly be the only way to proceed now," he said. "But tell me: what made you think of such an idea?"*

*The warrior replied, "We are not better or more valuable than the people we defend. We are all your subjects, and we must all recognize our humanity. Those of us who stand before you were all children once, and one day we will be old. We must give each one of your people an opportunity to live and to grow. If we are true warriors, we must suffer with our people."*

This young warrior understands that all people are connected. He sees himself (as well as his fellow warriors) in the people of his country. His heart is with the people because he knows that his heart *is* the heart of the people. This idea—which is also called empathy—is a basic part of courtesy. When we see that our weaknesses and fears and hopes are the same weaknesses, fears, and hopes of other people, we are planting the roots of courtesy. Then any outward sign of kindness or respect, such as a thoughtful word or action, comes directly from the inside—naturally and honestly.

Think about the times when you are most unhappy. In those times, do you ever feel all alone and deserted? Do you sometimes think that, even though you're trying your best, no one appreciates you or gives you any credit or respect?

## Room for Reflection

- What are some qualities of good losers and good winners? How might being both a good loser and a good winner show strength?

- You've probably encountered a few show-offs in your life. Why do you think people feel the need to boast about their accomplishments, or try to make others feel less worthy of their achievements?

- Think about the word *encourage*. What does it mean to you? How do you think it might take courage for a warrior to encourage someone else?

- Is being nice the same as being courteous? In what ways are these terms synonymous? In what ways are they not?

Now take a minute to think about how you feel when you realize that someone really cares about you. You probably feel a deep connection to that person. Sometimes, on a dark day, a friendly face can make it seem as though the sunshine has come back into your world. Perhaps you can be an encouraging voice for someone. You might brighten someone else's day with a kind word. By thinking about how you feel during your bad days and tough times, and then imagining yourself in others' shoes—by empathizing with the people around you—you may find ways to see beyond yourself and help a friend or classmate.

Empathy is often revealed when new students join Taekwondo classes. The newcomers are usually pretty nervous. They know that they have a lot to learn. Meanwhile, their fellow students all seem to know exactly what they are doing—and many are highly skilled. The experienced students who are the most courteous always offer to help the beginners and spend time encouraging them and talking with them. These students see themselves in the beginners. They remember how they were once confused and nervous, and they want to help make the new students feel comfortable and welcome.

This same kind of connection-making can happen in all kinds of classes, clubs, and social settings. We've all been the new person sometime, somewhere. We've all felt awkward and unsure. And we are all looking for acceptance and companionship. When we see ourselves in others and reach out to them with kindness and empathy, we put into action the courtesy that lives within the warrior's heart.

## A Story from the Warrior's Path

Sometimes you might wonder, "Why should I be courteous?" Well, just doing one little courteous thing could make someone else's day.

For example, one day at school after class everyone was walking through the door, rushing to get to the cafeteria. A girl was holding the door open for everyone. No one was paying attention to her. As my friend and I walked through the doorway, we said "Thanks" to the girl holding the door. She smiled and said, "You're welcome." I could tell the girl was happy that someone was courteous enough to say thank you to her.

Another time when I realized how courtesy could brighten someone's day, I saw a boy at school drop his books and folders. Some people just looked at him and laughed. Others started kicking his pencils down the hall. My friend went to retrieve his pencils while I bent over and helped him pick up his things. Once the boy had all of his things he looked up at us and said, "Thanks." I could tell that we made the boy happy just by doing that one little thing, and it made me feel like a better person.

Being courteous doesn't mean you have to write someone a thank-you note because that person held open a door for you or helped you pick up something you dropped. But doing one small courteous thing can make a difference. After all, when someone holds a door open for you, that person doesn't have to. He or she chooses to. This shows courtesy.

Now instead of asking, "Why should I be courteous?" start asking yourself, "How can I be courteous?"

—Naima, 13

## Closing Thoughts on Courtesy

Showing real courtesy—courtesy that is rooted in the heart, and which grows out of genuine respect—is a matter of strength. Sometimes it takes a warrior's courage to show authentic courtesy. In some cases, you could find that being courteous to all people can bring teasing from others. Other times you might find that your kind gestures are rejected or simply ignored, and that can hurt. At times like these, you might have second thoughts about living according to this principle.

But see if your kindness will eventually win out. Try reminding yourself that all people basically have the same needs. Warriors not only understand this idea, but embrace opportunities to help others fulfill their needs. There are many such opportunities each day. As a Korean proverb states, "A great river does not refuse any small streams." You might think of your courteous actions as the "small streams" that contribute to the "great river" of a more peaceful world.

You might also remember what Master Yi said: The "greatest enemy" is fear. Overcoming the fear of rejection can bring great results, not only for you but also for others. Or think back to the story of the young man who wanted all of the warriors to give up some of their food for the people. He was not afraid of how others would react to his suggestion—and he was confident that such kindness would make a difference. His deep respect was based on his knowledge and his strength. In turn, that strength gave him the courage to be courteous in a bold and meaningful way. Can you do the same?

*Sow much, reap much.*
*Sow little, reap little.*

Chinese proverb

# The Second Principle
# Integrity

On the second day, Master Yi led the student-warriors to the highest point behind the town. They climbed for over an hour, all of the young people helping their teacher along the way. When they reached the summit, the air was cooler, yet the sun breaking through the shifting clouds warmed their faces. They sat for a while, looking in all directions. They had climbed this small mountain many times before, but on this day, the air was special. It seemed to be a perfect mixture of the warm, moist air of the shore with the crisp, light air of the heights.

They remained silent for a long time, smiling and breathing peacefully. From where they were, they could see the hills meeting the plain, then the plain giving way to the shoreline.

At last, Master Yi swept his hand across the horizon, toward the land and then the ocean. He said, "If you care enough, you can see that all things come together to make a natural and beautiful world. And if you care enough, you can bring all the parts of yourself together to form a natural and beautiful self. This is integrity."

He closed his eyes and stretched out his arms. "Do you think you can tear your arms from your body or your fingers from your hand?" He shook his head and smiled. "Of course not. You must try to connect yourself, not separate. Let your mind know your heart and your heart know your mind."

Then Master Yi turned away from the group and pointed, tracing his finger along the path of a distant river that emptied into the sea. He continued, "The wholeness is all around you. See it. The child educates the parent as much as the parent educates the child. The smallest bird may sow a single seed, which gives root to the largest tree."

The largest and strongest student-warrior stood up and asked, "How does integrity concern our skill as warriors?"

Master Yi said, "As you develop and improve your technique and skill as warriors, you must develop and improve yourself, your whole self, your character and your mind. Make your inner self as strong as your outer self."

Another warrior, one whose musical skills as a flutist were well known in the town, stood up. She asked, "How will we know if we have achieved this integrity?"

The teacher appeared to have expected such a question. "When you do something well and do it naturally, or when you act according to your beliefs, then you have found integrity," he said. "But such moments of integrity may be short-lived if you do not keep striving for them at all times. So you must always work to join what you do with who you are. If your character is strong, then your actions will be strong, as well."

**2**

*Master Yi motioned for them all to stand, and then he said:*

Looking is good. Seeing is better. Listening is good.
Hearing is better. Hear this poem with your hearts:

Sometime as the sun goes down
walk with me into the woods,
where we will follow the trail
of our fathers.

You will see
a green finger of grass
beneath that patch of snow,
and the birth of color
in the white bark of the birch tree.

The round eye of an agate will squint at you
from the mud of the stream
before clarity washes everything clean.

Then you will see the truth:
All parts must come together.
Your thought marries your action,
your hand holds your mind,
and your own sharp sword
may soften into a song.

*As the master finished his lesson, the students stood qui-etly, letting their eyes take in the vastness, the wholeness below them—the foothills, the plain, the river, the shoreline, the sea, and the sky. They felt light and energetic. One of them began to hum a song they had once sung as children, and the flute player lifted her flute to her lips. Then the rest of the students broke into a harmonious melody as they followed Master Yi down the path.*

# Four Fundamentals for the **Warrior**

Warriors show integrity when they develop a strong personal moral code, and then try to live by the ideals of that code. There is a sense of honesty in this, as outward actions become signs of internal beliefs. Some people refer to this simply as character, and so a person of integrity is a person of character. In addition, Master Yi tells his students to live a "whole life." But what does it mean to live a "whole life"? One good way to think of integrity is to consider the word *integration*. To integrate means to bring together, not to separate. That means that warriors try to develop into well-rounded individuals who appreciate many different types of people and activities, and who try to grow in new ways. Warriors are eager and open-minded learners. As a modern warrior, you can begin to develop integrity by practicing these four fundamentals:

- Let your actions reflect your ideals.
- Let your positive thoughts bring about positive actions.
- Develop your body, mind, and spirit.
- Practice being still.

## Let Your Actions Reflect Your Ideals

Throughout your life, you've probably become familiar with certain values. Perhaps you've grown up in a home where diligence is valued, where one or both of your parents work very hard to keep the family well fed and housed. Maybe you once had a soccer coach who taught players to value teamwork. Perhaps you had a teacher who instilled in you the importance of honesty, or you've been involved in Scouting, where being trustworthy is expected.

Whatever your experience, you have been introduced to ideals that you may still embrace. But it isn't always easy to follow those ideals. Many temptations may draw us away from behaving according to our values. A story from the Won Hwa illustrates such a challenge.

*One year, during a happy and prosperous decade, King Jinheung asked the two Won Hwa, the female leaders of the kingdom's young elite, to prepare a special cultural festival for the people. This festival was supposed to feature dancing, recitations, singing, and music by the Hwarangdo. A prize, one horse from the royal stable, would go to the finest performer. The Won Hwa told their young students to begin preparing for the event, and they brought in some famous adult teachers to help the students improve in various arts. Naturally, the selected young people were honored and delighted to know they would be the featured performers at the kingdom's festival.*

*Every day, two of the young people, good friends, expressed their fervent hopes of winning the horse. One of them, a singer, practiced a difficult song that she knew would please the king. The other, an older boy, memorized and rehearsed a famous tale of bravery and honor among the king's guards. They often joked with each other, smiling, and saying, "That horse will be mine!"*

*Throughout the preparations, the Won Hwa reinforced the basic tenets of the Hwarangdo. One of these tenets was "Never retreat in battle." These young students had not yet confronted an enemy on the battlefield, so this ideal seemed distant and unreal to them. Nevertheless, they repeated it and enthusiastically included it as part of their code.*

*When the day of the festival arrived, many people gathered. The king, his family, and his subjects all rejoiced in the event. Many performances pleased the audience, but nothing brought such applause as the girl's song. Only one performance remained: the boy's recitation of the famous tale of bravery and honor. By the time he appeared, he was visibly shaken and somewhat fearful. He had practiced and practiced, but his friend's singing had moved him deeply—as it had the audience—and he felt sure that his own performance would be inferior. In the end, he performed admirably—but the girl's song still brought the greatest share of the king's praise, and she was awarded the magnificent horse.*

*The next day, when the young Hwarangdo gathered for their usual training, the girl brought the horse. Her peers rejoiced in her success, for it reflected well on them all. They were, after all, part of a special and privileged group. The boy was especially happy for his friend. Then, to everyone's surprise, the girl announced, "Yesterday, as I finished singing my song, I heard the applause and I felt certain that I had won the contest. But winning a contest is not part of our code. Winning a contest is not an ideal of ours. When I left the arena and saw my friend Jun Sung doubting his own abilities as he prepared to perform, I realized something about our code. 'Never retreat in battle' became clear to me. He could have backed away, knowing that the people had already voiced their approval of my performance—but instead he stepped forward. He performed with dignity and grace. He did not retreat, even though the result seemed already decided. And so, I hope he will share the prize with me. I won the contest, but he practiced our code."*

Have you ever encountered a situation where it would have been easier to value victory than to practice an ideal? Maybe you have had the opportunity to copy someone's work for a class in order to receive a good grade. Or perhaps you once found some money at the park, and you debated whether to turn it in or keep it for yourself. Do you know what your most important values are? Can you hold to those ideals even in the face of temptation? To live with integrity, a warrior must know the answers to these questions.

**2**

*Voice of a Warrior*

*"I choose to live my life with integrity because then people have more trust in me, and that opens up so many more opportunities in life."*

—Jacob, 16

## Let Your Positive Thoughts Bring About Positive Actions

When the Hwarangdo went into battle, they did so with positive thoughts. Warriors try not to think about defeat. They think, instead, about doing the right things and doing them well. Similarly, as you face your daily challenges, you may find that positive results will occur more often when you have positive thoughts. It even makes sense to put words to your thoughts. For example, saying, "I'm no good" doesn't carry any positive power. It may make you feel defeated before you even face a challenge. Instead, saying, "I can improve" is making a strong and positive statement. Your potential for success rests heavily on your ability and willingness to talk to yourself positively. Our words often become our actions—and success depends upon actions.

Sometimes it's not easy to think positively, though. We all grow discouraged at times. It may seem like you experience failure more often than success. Do you recall not believing that you'd ever be able to run a mile in gym class? Or wondering if others would accept you with your flaws *and* your strengths, whatever they might be? You're not alone if you have these worries and doubts. They're a normal part of being human. But warriors train themselves to think positively, and to truly believe that they can and will conquer any obstacle before them. Consider the difference between these statements: "I'll believe it when I see it," and "I'll see it when I believe it!" The first statement reflects doubt, while the second one shows confidence.

In the martial arts, a common "test" is the breaking of boards or other barriers with a kick or a punch. This not only signifies the student's ability to execute a technique with power, but also indicates something more important than physical skill—one's ability to face and overcome an obstacle. How might you face your own fears and doubts? If you've practiced hard and learned to believe in your skill, what sort of thoughts might go through your head when you're faced with an obstacle? Sometimes martial arts students view the board-breaking challenge as the most important part of their passage to a higher rank. It causes them to face the unknown and believe that they can accomplish their goal. Do you know how you would respond? If you think you can break one board, then how about two? Or three?

How do you train yourself to think positively, so that positive results are more likely to happen? It is important to realize that you must practice this way of thinking, especially if you often have thoughts that have the power to defeat you. Instead of complaining about a science test, you might say to yourself, "I may not be the best student in the class, but I'll do my very best on this test." Or if you're having a problem with one of your classmates or peers, you could say to yourself, "I don't know why she doesn't like me, but if I remain hopeful, things may change over time." Even if the results aren't what you desire, by thinking in this positive way, you're still working on building a warrior's heart. It's a hard road sometimes, but you may be surprised at your progress.

A good way to begin to think positively is to make a list of activities you don't like to do but that are

## Room for Reflection

- What do you think is one of the most important ideals that people can have? Why? What kinds of obstacles can prevent us from practicing this ideal, and how can we overcome them?

- Can you think of a recent situation in which one of your values was challenged? What happened? How did you respond?

- Think about a challenge that you're dealing with in some part of your life. How could positive thinking help you respond to this challenge?

- Master Yi mentioned "strong character" and "strong actions." What do you see as the relationship between them?

necessary. For example, perhaps you don't enjoy waiting for the bus, studying for a social studies class, or doing household chores. Next to each activity on your list, write down two benefits of doing it. Then write a sentence that reinforces the benefits and boosts your positive attitude. For example, "Waiting for the bus seems like a waste of time, but I get a chance to review my history homework and perhaps talk with someone I don't know very well." Or, "I really dread the thought of cleaning my room, but when I do it, I feel good about the fact that I'm helping out at home." Repeat these statements aloud, and post them in your room, locker, or notebook. Over time, this approach may help you develop the positive thinking that warriors possess. Sometimes we want immediate results, but try to be patient and stick with it.

## Develop Your Body, Mind, and Spirit

Warriors have a commitment to develop their "whole selves." Since we are full human beings—not just a collection of our individual traits and parts—we must be strong in more than one way. You are not just an athlete, or a student, or a singer. You are not just a friend, or a mechanic, or a dancer. You are *more*. You are a total person—and as a warrior, you can continue to develop yourself in important ways. Warriors know how to connect with the world. They appreciate different people and are interested in many things (even though they're probably not skilled at all of them). As you develop your warrior's heart, you may want to try out for a team, listen to many different kinds of music, learn more about computers, or enroll in a photography class. You can challenge yourself in many arenas.

Have you sometimes been reluctant to try something new because you thought you would fail or look foolish? Diving into the unknown demands bravery, and many people avoid trying new things because of fear. The warrior's heart can conquer fear. But where do you begin?

Start by looking around you at school and at home. Look at your classmates, family, and friends. Consider the many activities they participate in and what they like to do, as well as the things you enjoy doing. Now look beyond what you're familiar with. Pick out an activity that you've never done before but that you think you might like—and give it a try! It will be unfamiliar to you at first, and, yes—it might be intimidating or scary. But soon you may find that your fear begins to lessen. You may find yourself looking at the world differently as you challenge and develop yourself in new ways. As long as you're learning, you will never be a failure. You might even consider keeping track of your progress in a journal or diary. Later on, when you look back at what you've written, you might feel very differently about the activity.

An ancient story about two young men and a king shows the importance of being well-rounded and versatile, and of trying to keep a broad perspective.

The king needed a new bodyguard, so he advertised throughout the kingdom and held contests to find the best warrior to assume this great responsibility. All of these contests centered on physical skills such as hand-to-hand fighting. The final two contestants—both famous young men who had proven themselves to be loyal subjects as well as excellent soldiers—had each defeated many skilled warriors to reach this point in the competition. The king decided to give them one last test. "You may leave the arena," he said to the warriors. "Tomorrow I want you to appear at the palace with a gift."

As the sun rose the next day, the warriors appeared at the palace with their gifts. The first warrior stepped forward and bowed before the seated king as he said, "My king, I present you with my personal sword. I made this weapon with my own hands. I have heated it, forged it in the flames, and used it in battle. I have killed many of your enemies with it and chopped down some of the strongest trees in the land. There is no other sword like it." The warrior placed the sword at the king's feet.

The second young warrior stepped forward, bowed, and said, "My king, I present you with this sapling. If someone plants it outside the palace gates, you will see it from your throne, and your subjects will see it, too. It will one day grow into a giant oak, where many generations may enjoy its beauty and the shade of its strong branches." He laid the sapling, wrapped in a damp, muddy cloth, at the feet of the king.

The king considered the gifts before him for a few moments. Then, smiling, he stood up. He said, "Thank you for bringing these gifts. You are both fine subjects and excellent young warriors, and I have made my decision." To the first warrior, he said, "My friend, you are a great fighter, which you have proven to me in the arena and on the battlefield. Your sword is a great weapon—and it is greatest as a weapon in your hands. Thank you for your service. Please keep your sword and use it to protect our kingdom." To the second warrior, he said, "My friend, you also have proven to me that you are a great fighter. But today you have shown me something more—something very important. You understand beauty and life, not just destruction and death. Your gift of the tree shows me that you are more than a great fighter. You are also a young man of culture and refinement. You are a warrior with great strength and great soul—someone who loves all of my subjects and the future of our kingdom, not just me. You are my new bodyguard."

### Voice of a Warrior

*"Many people feel that if they go faster, their lives will have more meaning. But they should really slow down and just be alone and quiet once in a while."*

—Eva, 15

## Practice Being Still

One day an experienced leader of the Hwarangdo approached one of the younger warriors and said, "You have shown great courage in battle and a disciplined spirit in your training. Many of the other warriors cannot match your skill, nor your bravery. I am putting you in charge of 100 new recruits."

The young warrior was pleased. He had worked hard at his training, and others had told him that one day he might be promoted. He said to the leader, "I am honored that you are giving me this responsibility. Thank you." The leader continued, "Before you assume your duty, you must go away for one month. Go into the mountains. Take nothing with you, not even your sword. You know how to eat what the land provides. While you are there, listen to the mountain's sounds: the birds, the breeze, the running water. Smell the flowers and feel the soft grass. Reflect on the values of the Hwarangdo. Continue to train your body every day, and learn *from being alone. You need this time before you return to command the new warriors. Go now."*

*The younger man did not ask any questions. He bowed, turned, and set out for the mountains.*

Like this young warrior, all of us must take time to focus and prepare for the action in our lives. Consider the busyness of your own daily life. You go to school, spend time with friends, take part in clubs or sports, do homework, talk on the phone, and chat on the computer. Maybe you have a part-time job, or you volunteer at a local community center or homeless shelter. And those are just a few of your many activities! But part of integrity is learning to be still—to pause and take the time to assess our lives, think calmly, and gather the strength to make changes if we need to. In this very busy world with so much stimulation and activity, it's more important than ever to practice being still. Your stillness will allow you to connect with, acknowledge, and become more committed to your beliefs. It will help you get rid of the clutter in your life, recognize simplicity for a few moments, and then prepare you to act in focused ways when the time is right.

This stillness may also give you a chance to reflect on what you're doing with your life and to contemplate not only what you like about yourself, but also what you want to change. This takes great courage! Many people fill their lives with so much coming and going, so much activity, because they are afraid to look into themselves and to see something they don't like.

The older warrior in the story knew that when the younger warrior went off to spend time alone, the young man would be forced to look deeply at himself. He would come to know himself better, and in doing so he would become a better leader. As we know ourselves better, we also

2

know others better. As warriors, we want to be sure that when we act, our actions are grounded in our values, that they are deliberate actions, and that they are rooted in self-knowledge. Our self-knowledge grows in action, but it also thrives in stillness. Warriors are comfortable being alone with themselves and their thoughts.

So how can you attain this quality of the warrior? Try setting aside a half hour each day—the same time each day, if possible—to spend all by yourself. If you can, make this stillness "quiet time," too. Try not to play music or watch TV. Just *be.* You could sit in a quiet room or go for a walk in a city park. The important thing is that you get away from the usual activities and commitments of your daily life. By scheduling a time for this stillness, you make it a priority and you give it importance. During this time you might find that your mind will review the events of the day, or you may come up with an idea to improve a relationship. What is most important is that you try to set aside this time each day.

After you've done this for several days, do you find that it takes patience and strength to be alone and quiet with one's thoughts? Try not to be discouraged if you cannot calm yourself or you do not take a full half hour every time. Be patient with yourself, and try again the next day.

## Room for Reflection

- The Hwarangdo were well-rounded, versatile young people who trained their bodies, their minds, and their characters. If you were going to develop part of yourself, what part would you choose? What would be the first step you might take?

- If you were going to suggest that a new course or activity be offered at your school, what would it be? Why? How do you think you could help get it started?

- What is the greatest distraction to your "stillness"? Why is this thing so tempting?

- What is one of your fears? How might you overcome it?

## A Story from the Warrior's Path

In today's age, the life of the average kid can become extremely hectic. We must be able to manage our time with everything we do—from sports and other extracurricular activities to our family life and schoolwork. Trying to balance all of these activities can become stressful. If we think about all of the things we do as being separate and unrelated, then the lessons we learn and skills we gain from doing these things can seem useless and a waste of time. However, learning to integrate the lessons learned from different activities can improve not only how well we perform in specific parts of our lives, but also how well we can apply these skills to all aspects of our lives. We must follow the principle of integrity to truly apply all of our knowledge in everything we do.

Integrity is also a way of staying true to yourself and accomplishing what you feel is the right thing to do. For me, having integrity means using the "practice what you preach" method. When teaching others, people tend to tell the student what the best possible outcome would be if the student applied the maximum amount of effort. The teacher gives the student a goal, but in the end only the student can determine how hard he will work for what he wants. Students must show integrity in their work ethic if they want to achieve their goals. How students do their schoolwork at home is a reflection of how strongly they are willing to work for what they say they want. Having integrity is not just doing what is expected when someone is around, but doing more than what is expected when you are alone.

—Cory, 17

## Closing Thoughts on Integrity

Practicing integrity takes courage. It's sometimes very hard to stick to our personal ideals when we're tempted to abandon them. You might remember the girl who won the king's praise and the magnificent horse. She decided to share her prize because the boy had acted according to the warrior's code—he had not retreated in the face of difficulty or fear. Remember, too, that it takes strength to keep thinking positively in challenging situations. Negative thinking can defeat us even before we begin a task. It also requires bravery to try new things and face new challenges in order to develop yourself. And the last fundamental—"Practice being still"—can give you another great way to discover integrity—but it, too, can be tough. In stillness we must face ourselves—the good and the bad. True stillness lets us reassess our values, consider our deeds, and prepare ourselves for lives of action.

As you'll discover with all the principles of the warrior, you may occasionally stumble as you try to lead a life of integrity. Try not to expect perfection as you develop your personal values and strive to live by them. Continue to learn about yourself through your efforts, and then try to make your improvements into good habits. You'll likely see that you are developing your integrity through your consistent efforts. Which of this principle's four fundamentals do you think will be the most challenging for you?

One can build a mountain by
collecting specks of dust.

Korean proverb

# The Third Principle
## Perseverance

The next day dawned cool and damp, with a light rain falling. Despite the chill, Master Yi woke the students early and took them to the forest. The young people had always loved the forest with its thick trees and vibrant wildlife. But everything looked heavy and dark to them now. Water dripped from the leaves and ferns, from the thin branches and the rough bark of trees. Everyone was very tired by the time they left the path and came into a clearing, where fallen tree trunks and boulders rested. The scene seemed eternal, as if it had never been disturbed. The teacher pointed to the logs and rocks, motioning for the young people to sit. They wondered why he smiled, even as the universe appeared to be crying and while they were so uncomfortable—scalps soaked by rain, and their clothes hanging on their cold bodies like grief.

Master Yi spoke calmly. "No real lesson is easy. Not every breath can be a smooth one. On this cool and rainy day, you want to sleep in your beds and dream of the warm sand of the beach. You want to lie down, extend your hand, and ask the world for a gift."

He took a slow, deep breath and went on. "The gift of the world is a seed—life—but after you accept it, your hand must be ready to plant it and cultivate it. You must take care of it so the

3

seed does not dry up or become food for the sparrow. And you must nurture this seed every day, not just on the warm, bright days when you feel content."

He paused. He stretched his arms wide, opening his hands and then closing them into fists. "Your greatest power is not in the quickness of your feet or in the strength of your arms." Then he tapped his forehead gently and touched one finger to his lips. "It is not in the skill of your mind or in the sugar of your tongue. The trickle does not become a stream in a day. The stream does not become a river in a year. The river does not carve a canyon in a lifetime."

Master Yi fell silent, and one of the girls—one whom the others always respected for her determination—stood up. After fidgeting nervously for a moment, she asked, "But Master Yi, why have you brought us here on this rainy morning to hear these words? Couldn't you just as easily have given us this lesson inside, where it is dry and we can listen better?"

The teacher nodded. He understood. He replied, "In fact, this morning is perfect for what I must remind you of: You know the hardship of training, but hardship will be with you for all of your years. When I leave you, hardship will continue. When you leave one another, hardship will continue. When you are old, hardship will continue. You must accept and embrace the difficulty and persevere in action, not only in words. You must not give up or despair."

Then he looked at one of the older warriors beside him, someone who had studied with the master for many years. Master Yi put his hand on the student's shoulder and continued, "The sword

**3**

becomes strong when it is placed not once, not twice, but many times into the fire. And the heat alone does not strengthen it. The warrior pounds the hot metal with the stone or the hammer, again and again, to build the sword into a worthy weapon. You, too, must practice repetition, even when you are discouraged."

The girl who had spoken earlier asked another question. She was inquisitive and eager, but also slightly frustrated. "Teacher, how much must we repeat our actions and our lessons?"

Master Yi took a few steps back and forth before he answered. Then he stopped and said, "Do you hear the song of that bird? The song becomes more beautiful when you listen to it day after day and learn it by heart. Then you carry the song with you wherever you go. It is part of you. Did you learn to walk by taking one step? When you fell down, you got up and tried again until you could take one step, then two . . . and soon enough, you could walk without thinking. You were not discouraged by your failure."

"Remember this," he said. "Time teaches us if we let it. You may be strong for the moment, but the world turns. Keep training. Keep practicing. Keep learning."

He motioned for the students to stand, and then he said:

Looking is good. Seeing is better. Listening is good. Hearing is better. Hear this poem with your hearts:

We have followed the tracks in the snow.
There in the distant field,
beyond the icy creek,
the warriors motion us forward,
their naked arms making circles
against the gray sky,
the cold nothing but an idea.

It is here that we reach ourselves.
The truth of every breath we have ever taken
freezes on the wind above our heads.
Our bare feet are made
to take us farther,
deeper into our minds,
beyond what we thought we could be.

**3**

Master Yi had finished his lesson. He nodded his head and turned away from his pupils. Then he walked slowly out of the clearing, leaving the students to quietly contemplate their surroundings of soggy logs and damp rocks. When they realized he would not wait for them—that he had intentionally left them by themselves to ponder his words—they wandered out of the clearing after their teacher. As they did so, a few slanting rays of the morning sun broke through the wet branches and glistened on the leaves overhead.

# Four Fundamentals for the **Warrior**

The teacher's words about perseverance remind the students that they will face difficulties and hardship in their lives. These are tough reminders for anyone to hear. We all hope our lives will be smooth and happy. And warriors' lives may indeed be happy, but much of their happiness is the result of their consistency and hard work—the result of their perseverance. Warriors practice their skills regularly, and they endure frustrations along the way. The lessons that they learn by not giving up are lessons that will help them throughout life, in many circumstances. As a modern warrior, you might want to think of perseverance as a combination of patience and action. Developing patience will enable you to endure, and maintaining action will keep your warrior's heart strong. Here are four fundamentals to help you display the perseverance of a warrior:

- Focus on the present.
- Welcome hardship.
- Dig deep.
- Embrace repetition.

## Focus on the Present

Two common problems tend to crop up for people who forget to focus on the present. The first obstacle is that they may become impatient when they don't achieve the results they hope for. The second is that they may have trouble staying enthusiastic about what they're doing. Focusing on the present—the now—helps the warrior maintain the discipline necessary to reach a goal. The best warriors understand the importance of setting a goal for the future, and then focusing on the steps they must take—right now—toward achieving it.

When warriors are training, they aren't thinking constantly about their goal. They just train. They realize that if they do something long enough, they *will* become better at it. Positive results *will* follow. Warriors also understand that if they look too far ahead, they may not put their best effort into what they're doing at that moment. Their skill doesn't come from thinking about it, but from practice and perseverance. Have you found that you improved at something when you really enjoyed doing it? Did you lose track of time when you were involved?

A high school track coach often tells the story of a terrific high jumper. When the girl was born, her parents planted the seeds of a hedge around their house. Shortly after the little girl could walk, she started to hop over the hedge, which had grown to be about 2 inches tall. When the hedge was nearly a foot tall, the girl was 5 years old—and she was still jumping it, many times every day, just for fun. As she grew up, so did the hedge. And she kept on jumping every day, until, as a teenager, she could do a high jump over a hedge that was more than 5 feet tall. Onlookers often expressed amazement and asked the girl how she'd learned to jump so high. She answered them simply. "Ever since I could walk, I've been jumping that hedge—except it wasn't as tall then as it is now. At first, it was tiny. It kept growing, just as I did. And I never stopped jumping."

The coach tells this story to remind his athletes that they must train if they want to improve. But if they treat every day as a new challenge—and especially if they can find some fun in the challenge—they'll be aware of the moment, not get too preoccupied with the future, and stay enthusiastic about their training.

Think about the ways this idea might affect your life. For example, say you're facing a challenge in a tough class. You might wonder if you can ever grasp the concepts that the teacher asks you to master. But instead of worrying about the end of the school term, try to focus on what you have to do each day. This won't suddenly make everything simple. You'll still have a challenge ahead of you. But one day, you'll realize that you've taken many steps along the way toward your goal. You might not be all the way there yet, but you're making progress—one day at a time. Or perhaps you want to learn how to play the guitar. As you're first beginning to learn, try to concentrate on the here and now of simple chords and basic techniques—not on the complicated song you hope you'll be able to play one day. Face the challenges right in front of you, and maintain focus on them. Then, like the high jumper, you'll improve day by day.

Your ability to focus on the present will put you in the warrior class. Warriors practice regularly, and they practice well. They devote their energy, their minds, and their bodies

## Voice of a Warrior

*"A principle that I firmly live by is perseverance, because I never give up when things become difficult. For example, I have tried for my black belt twice and haven't been able to pass . . . but I haven't stopped trying and I won't stop trying."*

—Sophia, 18

to the task at hand. They know that, if they do this, positive results will follow. Do you think that you can set a long-term goal and then focus daily on the steps to achieve it? Will you be tempted to think too far ahead, and will the steps bore you? Or will you find some pleasure in making progress every day?

## Welcome Hardship

The members of the Hwarangdo trained themselves in amazing ways. How many people do you know who swim in freezing rivers or run barefoot in the snow? That's what these young warriors did. They "welcomed hardship." They willingly placed themselves in difficult situations so that they could endure other hardships in their lives, including those unrelated to battle. They knew that if they could train in hard conditions day after day, they would be able to withstand very challenging circumstances, and they could persevere in the face of terrible trials.

A great and highly respected martial artist named Master Han often told the tale of his own test of perseverance. He decided to challenge himself by practicing one punch for 14 hours a day for two weeks. During that time, he did not practice any other techniques—only that one punch, with each hand, from one particular position. Master Han's main challenge was not physical. It was mental. Master Han "welcomed hardship," and he decided that he would not give up. With that kind of experience, he was unlikely to give up on anything worthwhile in the future.

Here's a question that you might ask yourself as a warrior: Do I want to take the easy way, or the way that will make me stronger? The temptation is often to take the easy way, isn't it? Some students are tempted to cheat on tests or to take something from a book or website and claim the idea as their own. Some students in a gym class, if asked to run four laps, will run three because it's easier. But the easy way does not usually build the warrior's heart. It may even break us down by allowing us to become accustomed to looking for the easiest path. Then, when we face a truly difficult task, we're not prepared. We're not confident in our ability to succeed.

Maybe, like many teens, you've had a job during the summer or after school. Perhaps you've worked mowing lawns, waiting tables at a restaurant, or teaching swimming lessons. While you may like some aspects of the work (the smell of the freshly cut grass, the pleasure of serving good food to happy customers, or the satisfaction of teaching a new swimming technique to an eager student), there are likely parts of the job that you'd rather not do. This is where your opportunity to welcome hardship comes in. It's fairly easy to do the work that you enjoy, but would you consider volunteering to do some of the work that's harder, or that you don't enjoy as much? Would you offer to do your least favorite task, whether it's changing the oil in your customers' lawnmowers, taking a few weekend shifts at the restaurant, or cleaning the locker room at the swimming pool? These are opportunities to welcome hardship. Seek hardship, and you may find that you're building your perseverance and your warrior spirit.

## Room for Reflection

- In what tasks or activities are you especially impatient? Can you think of reasons you're so impatient? How can you approach a task so you focus on the present and don't look too far ahead?

- What is the relationship between enthusiasm and one's ability to focus on the present? What are some helpful tactics to help you remain enthusiastic in your responsibilities?

- If you're going to welcome hardship in one part of your life, what might you have to sacrifice in another area?

Other ways to welcome hardship present themselves frequently, as well. All you have to do is put yourself in a challenging situation so that you can build perseverance. Perhaps you can do extra math problems, especially some difficult ones, from a homework assignment. Or maybe you'll decide not to watch TV for a month so that you can run a mile or two in the evenings. If you choose to welcome this sort of hardship, how do you feel after you've done it for a while? Do you notice any changes in the way you approach other tasks in your life, or in the attitude you have about yourself?

## Dig Deep

Do you remember some of the stories you read or heard during your childhood? Some of those stories are full of characters meant to teach us lessons. Do you remember any stories featuring main characters who succeed because of perseverance and hard work? Some of these characters show that they can call upon parts of themselves that they never knew existed. They "dig deep" at a time when they really think they've reached their limits. One of the most famous stories is *The Little Engine That Could*—the tale of an old, tired train engine that somehow makes a difficult journey to the top of a mountain. All of the other modern engines have the power and the equipment to make the trip easily, but the little old engine just keeps chugging away, tapping into some internal resource, until the goal is reached. Over and over, the engine repeats to itself, "I think I can! I think I can!"

Have you ever found—in a very difficult circumstance or time in your life—that your warrior's heart came alive when you thought you couldn't go on? Sometimes we surprise ourselves with the power that we have, just when we think it's time to give up. The warrior's motivation is available to everyone. The key is to remind ourselves that we have it. It may be another burst of energy, or a fresh image of success that launches us to keep going with enthusiasm. But all real warriors know that they have a powerful motivation inside of them—and they can call upon it when they need to. It is a sign of their bravery and strength.

In the early 1970s, a young soldier named Ron returned to the United States from fighting in the Vietnam War. He came home badly wounded. A land mine had exploded near him, and pieces of shrapnel had lodged themselves in his legs and spine. His legs didn't work the way they used to. When he entered Master Han's Taekwondo school, he was using two canes and could only shuffle his feet slowly. Nevertheless, he signed up for martial arts lessons.

At first, Ron did his exercises and practiced his techniques from the floor, where he could move more easily. Then, still holding himself upright using his strong arms and his canes, he began to stand and lift his legs to kick. After months of daily practice, he finally broke a board by kicking it. And after three years of regular practice, Ron passed his black belt test.

Ron taught everyone around him about perseverance. He especially demonstrated what it means to "dig deep." When he first decided to try the martial arts, he may not have known what he was capable of. But as he achieved each small goal, he realized he had an amazing power deep within himself, an internal force that allowed him not only to keep going, but also to reach new heights.

All of us have activities in which we wish we could perform better. Perhaps you wish you could inspire others with your piano playing, make new friends more easily, or score more points for your basketball team. Perhaps you wish you

**3**

had more energy or enthusiasm in your daily life. It's not easy to "dig deep" when we are discouraged or uninspired. Can you identify an activity at which you want to do better? Can you think of a saying that will help you focus and build your enthusiasm when you feel disheartened?

## Voice of a Warrior

*"Perseverance means to keep going when you don't think you're strong enough. It's trying hard anyway, even if you think that you've finally hit rock bottom. It means not being satisfied until your goal is met."*

—Jasmine, 14

## Embrace Repetition

Ron, Master Han, and the girl who became a great high jumper demonstrated amazing perseverance. They were not superhuman. They were human beings who became discouraged or unmotivated at times, just like all of us do. Yet they all shared one very important quality: they practiced repetition. They could not have succeeded without repeating their actions over and over.

In some ways, you do the same thing. You get out of bed and go to school five days a week throughout the school year. Maybe you practice the same music piece over and over, or take the dog for a walk every single night. While it's true that your parents and other people expect some of these things from you, they don't go through the school day with you, do they? They can't memorize for you the music you're learning. *You* are the one practicing perseverance through your repetition.

The hard part for all of us comes when we must embrace repetition in order to succeed at something—and we just don't feel like doing it. For example, you might not feel like going to school every day, or studying vocabulary homework over and over again, or washing the dishes every night. And when there's no one standing over you, demanding that you do something, it's hard to keep going. Sometimes you might have to remind yourself that the very act of repeating something worthwhile makes you stronger. You are building patience and the warrior's heart through your repetition.

An old story about a brother and his younger sister who wanted to learn from a great martial arts teacher reveals the value of embracing repetition. When the two children came to the master and asked if he would teach them, he said, "First, each of you take a sponge and a bucket of water and scrub the floor. When you are finished, come see me." It took the boy and the girl three hours to scrub the floor. When they came back to the teacher, he said, "Good. Now put the sponges and bucket away and come see me again tomorrow."

When the brother and sister returned the next day, the teacher had them scrub the floors again. This went on for a month, until the brother burst out, "When are you going to teach us martial arts?" The teacher replied, "Don't worry. Just scrub the floor." After the second month of doing the same job day after day, the boy decided not to clean ever again. He never came back. But his sister kept going to the teacher and cleaning the floor—every day.

3

After a full year, the teacher told the girl to stop cleaning. He said, "Now I will teach you the martial arts techniques you wish to learn. But you have already learned the most important lesson of all—how to do something over and over again. You cleaned the floor and cleaned the floor and cleaned the floor. I know you will be a good student of mine because you will practice over and over again the things that I show you."

## Room for Reflection

- What is one time in your school day during which you often become discouraged? What can you do to encourage yourself?

- Can you think back to an event or activity where you truly had to "dig deep" in order to keep going? What motivated you then?

- To embrace repetition suggests that someone has a certain attitude about repeating a task. What sort of attitude would allow you to "embrace" any task you choose?

- What's one of your personal strengths, and how can you use it? What's one of your shortcomings, and what steps might you take to overcome it?

## A Story from the Warrior's Path

When I started learning Taekwondo, one of the first things I learned was the set of principles: courtesy, integrity, perseverance, self-control, indomitable spirit, community service, and love. Later, I came to realize that I had been practicing these ideas long before starting my training in martial arts.

For example, I remember taking driver's ed in high school. When the permits were handed out, I laughed at the expiration date on mine. I was thinking, "What kind of person would ever need to renew one of these? It couldn't take *that* long to get a license."

I would soon learn that I would be one of those people. I started learning how to drive with my identical twin brother. Unlike him, I have several challenges, both physical and otherwise, that made learning everything from walking to riding a bike—and now driving—more difficult. I was told it would take me twice as long as my brother to acquire the skill. I spent what seemed like forever practicing, driving with my parents every chance I got, and I tasted the bitterness of defeat when I failed the driving exam twice. In the end, what took my brother several months and a single driver's test took me five years, three learner's permit renewals, and three driving tests. I cannot deny that I was angry at my failure the first time, but I reasoned that plenty of people had failed a driver's test the first time. When I failed the test the second time, I became discouraged. After all, I simply wanted what everyone else seemed to have, and couldn't figure out why such a basic thing would be denied to me. Through this struggle I came to learn that if I truly wanted success, I had a choice: to continue to try or to give up completely. I chose to try, and on the third test I passed and got my license. All of my hard work had been worth it.

Now that I've been training in Taekwondo, I tend to view these kinds of trials like board breaks. Sometimes when you go to break your board, you succeed. Other times you don't. But the challenge will still be there, and if you have an attitude of perseverance you will choose to pursue the challenge until you attain success. You do not necessarily have to be or have been a martial artist to find the principles alive in your life, but like a martial artist you must look for and be open to their influence.

—David, 20

## Closing Thoughts on Perseverance

Perseverance is one of the most important qualities of a warrior. It involves both patience and action, and there can be no improvement without it. When you feel like giving up, it might help you to keep in mind that you can practice perseverance little by little, until you feel your warrior's heart getting stronger. Step by step. Step by step. How do you feel when you make even a small improvement?

Remember: there is no shortcut. Warriors are able to practice and practice whatever it is they want to become good at. They practice until what they are doing comes to them almost automatically. They practice until their practice becomes a habit. And they understand that the disciplined process of training for something—not the goal they wish to achieve—is what truly creates the warrior's heart.

You also might want to think about the first words of the fundamentals for this principle: *focus, welcome, dig,* and *embrace*. Each word suggests that in order to truly practice the principle of perseverance, you'll have to look at the challenge, whatever it is, with a single-minded, positive attitude. In our lives, we encounter many situations and forces that may tempt us to think negatively. And, as human beings, we're far from perfect, so we stumble along the way. Can you be prepared to deal with those distractions so that you can maintain a positive warrior spirit? What is a skill you would like to improve? Can you arrange your own practice schedule and stick to it—embracing repetition?

*He who kicks a stone in anger*
*hurts his own foot.*

Korean proverb

**4**

# The Fourth Principle
# Self-Control

On the fourth day, the students gathered behind their teacher's house, where he had a peaceful garden and a beautiful pear tree. Master Yi often spent hours in his garden, tending the flowers and watching the birds as they moved in the branches of the pear tree. He had taught the students that they could learn much about life by observing nature and by thinking about their place in the world. While they sat with him on this day, he said nothing for the longest time. But his eyes moved quickly. He watched the leaves and the branches, the flowers and the insects, the clouds and the birds.

At last Master Yi smiled and spoke. "Do you think about how much is going on here? The birds move in the sky. Some of them disappear while others land in the tree and sing for us. The plants grow, it seems, when we are not looking. The sun warms the earth, but we cannot see how it does so."

The teacher bent over and touched a patch of grass at his feet. Then he stood and spread his arms. He continued, "The life from the sun and the ground feeds the flowers and the trees and the grass, but we do not see how all of this happens. So much seems invisible to us. But we know that many truths affect everything that lives." He paused and then continued. "Do you think that the tree hates the nighttime? Is the bee upset when the flower dries up? Does one blade of grass speak harshly to its taller neighbor?"

Master Yi let his eyes wander over the faces of his students. Then he leaned forward slightly. "Are you different when the wind blows?" he asked. "Do you hate the flower when it dies? When the dove stops singing, do you change? I remind you today to feel the wind but not to let it rule your life, to enjoy the sun but not to let it change your mood, to smell the blossoms but not to despair when they blow away."

At that moment, a soft breeze passed through the garden. Several of the students closed their eyes, enjoying the sensation. When the breeze had ceased, Master Yi went on. "Know yourself. When you act, remember that no one acts for you. Every action is your own, so make every action the best one."

One of the younger students stood up and said, "Teacher, we are warriors. We will never let anything affect us. We are hard and fearless. Nothing will influence us if we don't want it to."

The teacher nodded, saying, "Yes, I know you can be hard and fearless. But you are also human. The hard, dry limb breaks in the storm. The unripe fruit is hard—but so is the withered fruit. Do not let your hardness cause you to break or die. And do not let hard words or cruel actions wither your soul."

Master Yi opened and closed one hand. "Your fist is yours to strike with. But the same hand caresses a child." He raised a foot briefly off the ground, saying, "Your feet are yours to kick with, but the same feet carry you to the side of a loved one. Your mouth yells in battle, but the same mouth sings a song. Self-control is not about hardness and toughness only. It is about knowing and understanding, seeing and thinking and believing. It is about being disciplined and also being human."

Master Yi took a step closer to the group of students and gazed affectionately at them, tilting his head slightly. Then he said, "When you know yourselves, you will act in the best way. You will move and speak in the best way. You will know what is best, and you will do it without question. And you may learn wisdom. Remember that the pretend warrior tries to conquer others, while the real warrior tries to conquer the self."

He motioned for the students to stand and come close to him. Then he said:

Looking is good. Seeing is better. Listening is good. Hearing is better. Hear this poem with your hearts:

You have been beneath the clouds,
when the rain cools your fiery words
and the discipline of the earth shows you the path,
welcoming your feet, your chosen steps.

You are there again now,
thinking clearly with one mind,
before you soar into the skies of decision,
amazing even the birds with your freedom.

This is you at your very best, knowing
that what you choose is who you are,
and then rising
and rising.

After Master Yi had finished speaking, he stood very still, raising his eyes to look at the branches of the pear tree. When a goldfinch darted from a low branch to a higher one, followed by its mate, he nodded and smiled. As the finches chattered to one another, the teacher and his students left the garden together, listening to the birdsong above them.

# Four Fundamentals for the Warrior

Master Yi hopes his students will see that self-control is an essential characteristic of the warrior. True warriors understand that they may not always be able to control what happens to them, but they *can* control how they respond to any situation. They respond with confidence and self-knowledge, understanding that without self-control they may live a chaotic or fearful life. They believe in their ability to respond wisely and well. You may find that self-control is very difficult to achieve—and it's even more difficult to practice consistently. Here are four fundamentals to help you on your way:

- Take responsibility.
- See the big picture.
- Choose discipline.
- Start with the little things.

## Take Responsibility

*The 17-year-old warrior had proven himself in battle, and he had shown his willingness to develop himself further by learning to play the flute, practicing calligraphy, and obediently serving his superiors. Through all of his training, he had been a cheerful and eager young man, as well as a courageous warrior. His fellow warriors respected him. One day, word circulated among the warriors that one of them would be sent on a dangerous mission to deliver a secret message to an opposing general. If the message got through to the general, a war—sure to cost many lives—could be avoided. The young warrior approached his leader and asked if he could be the one to take on the assignment.*

*"I do not think I can send you," the leader said after the young warrior had made his request. "You may have shown your capabilities, but I know about your family history. Your uncle and father have both been in prison, one of them for murder and the other for robbery. Am I right?" The young warrior said, "Yes, sir. In fact, I believe that both of them are still in jail." The leader nodded and continued, "Your family is not respected. While you have proven yourself in some ways, I fear there must be some large weakness within you. I cannot trust you with this mission."*

*The young warrior was saddened by this response, but he did not let his leader's opinion discourage him. He stood tall and said calmly, "I respect your decision not to let me go. But please do not make that decision based on something I did not do. I am not responsible for the actions of my father and my uncle—and they are not responsible for my actions. I am unhappy that my family must endure this disgrace. But if I have proven that I am worthy to undertake the mission, I hope you will allow me to deliver the message. I alone am responsible for what I do."*

This warrior has embraced the first fundamental of self-control. All warriors know that they are responsible for what they think, what they say, and what they do. They do not blame others. Instead, they think of ways that they themselves can act to make things better. They believe in their ability to make positive things happen through their thoughts, words, and actions.

When people assume responsibility for what they do and who they are, they can be strong when others try to damage them with their words and their actions. They can rely upon their inner strength to move forward. And when they make mistakes, they can admit them and then go on to improve.

This is a hard fundamental to grasp and to put into practice, especially when we may be personally responsible for an undesirable situation. Even if others have also been at fault and have tried to hurt us, we may still benefit from considering our own responsibility for what has happened. Still, we often prefer to look at others rather than at ourselves. Have you ever pointed your finger at someone else and ignored the role *you* played in a disagreement? Have you ever not listened to someone else in an argument because you were so certain that you were right? It's human nature to be stubborn and proud sometimes, rather than accept responsibility.

The next time things don't go the way you'd like, try to take a good, honest look at the situation and your role in it. If you can do this, then you're demonstrating your willingness to accept responsibility. Without being overly hard on yourself and thinking poorly of yourself, just sit back and consider what you could have done to help you get your desired result. Ask yourself this question: "If I get a second chance at this, what can I change about myself or my actions to get the results I want?"

## See the Big Picture

At age 14, Zoe was eager for more independence from her parents. Around her own house, she also longed for greater privacy. But both of these wishes appeared to Zoe to be out of reach. She felt as though her mother was always asking her questions, and her two younger brothers were often rowdy and noisy. Zoe's greatest frustration of all centered on her family's rules about using the computer. She desperately wanted her own computer in her room, away from the household's chaos and interruptions—but her mother insisted that she use the family computer in the living room.

Zoe, sometimes growing very emotional and angry, asked her mother again and again why she couldn't have her own computer in a private place. Her mother always answered her the same way, saying, "There are too many temptations online. I want you to be out in the open where you won't be tempted to look at things you shouldn't, and where you can ask me if you see something that bothers or confuses you. You're just too young right now, Zoe. Maybe in another year or so we can talk about it again." But Zoe wasn't satisfied with her mother's answer. She remained frustrated and upset.

One day, Zoe's nine-year-old brother told her about a new friend of his, an older boy who lived down the street. The boy went to Zoe's school, and she knew that he'd been suspended for fighting. Worried about her brother, she told him that the other boy was too old for him to hang out with. She told him that she thought the older boy might be a bad influence.

Zoe realized that she wanted to protect her brother from making a poor decision. Although her brother felt sure that he was responsible enough to be friends with the older boy, Zoe was still concerned about him. And suddenly, as she thought about her concern, she saw her mother's perspective. Even though Zoe believed she could act responsibly with a private computer, she began to understand her mother's desire to watch out for her welfare— just as she herself was watching out for her brother.

## Room for Reflection

- Can you think of a way you might improve a situation at school, at home, or among your peers? Can you bring people together in a positive way?

- What's one quality or tendency in yourself that you'd like to change or improve? If you make some improvements, will you achieve any positive effects in your relationships or in your ability to achieve a goal you have?

- In what areas of your life are you patient? In what areas might you need more patience?

- When do you most often find yourself getting angry? In those situations, what needs of yours are not being met?

Something about Zoe's outlook had changed—and she showed a very important quality of the warrior. She saw the "big picture." Because she could see her mother's perspective, she felt more able to look past her own wishes and see the situation from different angles. She also saw that her personal frustrations would eventually pass. She began to believe that, with time and patience, she might eventually get her wish for a computer in her room if she showed her mother that she was trustworthy.

Have you found that it can be extremely difficult to see the big picture? It seems that patience and practice are absolutely necessary for living by this fundamental. Maybe you've also found that you can't "force" yourself to control a situation, especially when you don't get what you want. Sometimes the more we try to force something to happen, the less successful we are. We can easily start to lose sight of the main issue. You might try to look at it from this perspective, if you can: "Whatever's happening at this difficult moment will make me stronger and wiser." Do you think you can see most experiences in life not as trials, but as opportunities? You might find that with an approach like that, your actions will more often be positive. Be patient with yourself if you don't always respond calmly. Keep trying.

When we're upset, hurt, or angry, we all have a hard time seeing the big picture. We tend to turn inward, focusing on ourselves and dwelling on the negatives of the situation. We may say, "Why me?" or, "This is as bad as it gets!" or, "I'm *never* going to get over this." It's rarely easy to look on the bright side when we're feeling bad or we're facing a difficult situation. Maybe a more helpful way to deal with things that make us angry or upset is to try to consider our own and other people's needs. The warrior knows the self, and he or she knows that, as human beings, we all have the same needs. We may express them in productive ways, or we may not. What are some of your most important needs as a person? Acceptance? Respect? Independence? Appreciation? (These are just a few of the needs that all people have.) If someone in your life frustrates you now, what might some of his or her needs be? Do you think you might understand why he or she often acts a certain way?

**Voice of a Warrior**

*"Self-control allows you to resist your impulses of the moment and to take the course of action that will be most beneficial to you in the long run."*

—Hiro, 18

## Choose Discipline

All warriors look at discipline as a choice, not as something that's forced upon them. They believe that what they choose determines who they are. And most often, they choose to act so they and others benefit in the long run. That's what discipline is: a consistent ability to act in a way that is good for us. Warriors aren't interested in feeling good for the moment. They want to do what they see as right, and what they believe will bring the best results. They take pride in knowing that their character is largely the result of their discipline, and they know that their discipline gives them power over their greatest enemy—themselves.

Have you found that you have a certain desire that tends to get in the way of your goals? For example, maybe you're a big fan of old science fiction movies, but the best time to see those films on TV is late on weeknights. Many times you just can't resist staying up to watch, which means that you don't get to sleep until after midnight. Then you're groggy and tired as you go through your school day and participate in after-school activities. What can you do? Maybe you don't want to give up your desire completely. But maybe you also feel somewhat powerless at times to control that desire.

Time management is an area of discipline that a lot of us struggle with. If it's difficult for you, try making a weekly schedule and stick to it every day for a certain period of time. Perhaps your after-school schedule could look something like this:

### Monday–Thursday

| | |
|---|---|
| 3:00–4:00 pm | Exercise |
| 4:00–4:30 | Go home; eat a snack |
| 4:30–6:00 | Do homework |
| 6:00–6:45 | Eat supper |
| 6:45–7:00 | Help clean up |
| 7:00–8:30 | Do homework |
| 8:30–10:30 | Do any chores; have free time |
| 10:30 | Record a movie; go to bed |

### Friday

| | |
|---|---|
| 3:00–4:00 pm | Exercise |
| 4:00–4:30 | Go home; eat a snack |
| 4:30 | The weekend! Watch the recorded movies, hang out with friends and family, study, etc. (Be sure to be in bed by 10:30 Sunday.) |

Of course, you have to set up the plan that works for you. And time management is just one sort of discipline. Maybe you love sweets or other unhealthful foods, and you've noticed that what you're eating is causing you to feel less sharp and energetic. Can you find a way to control your desire and not let it control you? For example, what if you tried to only eat these tempting foods three times a week or less, and also committed to choosing more healthful foods at other times?

If you struggle with any urge that may not be healthful or helpful—and most of us do, at least some of the time—you have a tremendous opportunity to show an important quality of all warriors. Warriors choose to make the decisions that are good for them, and they don't allow their desires to control them. They put themselves into situations where they can thrive. Certainly there will be times when you don't feel like sticking to your regimen, but do your best. Remember that all warriors face temptations. And there will be times when—like all warriors—you stumble or you fail to follow the rules you've set for yourself. But keep trying. Can you choose self-discipline over self-indulgence more often than not?

Here is a saying that may help you as you work on choosing discipline:

When warriors say *no* to harmful things, they say *yes* to their happiness.

## Start with the Little Things

*After a long time of peace in the kingdom, one year the Hwarangdo suddenly found themselves facing nearly constant threats from their country's larger neighbors. As always, the warriors had all been training very hard to stay ready for such a situation. But now the tension was mounting, and a group of* warriors was preparing to travel to the outer reaches of their territory. There, they would wait for an expected attack. On the day of their departure to the remote border, one very new warrior looked ready for battle. He had his sword sharpened, and his eyes shone with enthusiasm and determination. But when his superior asked him to step aside, he knew he was in for a great disappointment.

"You must stay behind this time," the leader told him.

"Why, sir?" the young warrior asked.

His superior replied, "You must practice more discipline. You have been training with the others, but I have noticed that you wait for someone else to do the work of cleaning up our village or helping with daily chores. You do not volunteer to tend to the horses or to wash the clothes of the senior warriors. These small acts are important because they show you are able to take care of the details in life. In order to deal with life-and-death situations with discipline and control, you must first be capable of dealing well with everyday matters. Stay behind this time and show that you can manage other tasks—cleaning, preparing food, and tending to your personal appearance and presentation better. Then we will see if you are ready for other tasks."

## Room for Reflection

- What does balance in life mean to you? What do you think you might need to achieve greater balance in your own life?

- Can you name one activity in your life that is very healthy for you? Is there one that is not so healthy?

- What do you see as the relationship between freedom and self-discipline?

- How might self-control give you more power in your life?

At first, this young warrior did not understand that the root of self-control lies in our everyday actions, not in the big event. He was eager for battle—but he let his enthusiasm overshadow his self-discipline. As a modern warrior, you, too, might choose to practice by challenging yourself with smaller things.

As you know, choosing discipline can be very difficult—especially when we are tempted to satisfy our every wish right away, or when we want to avoid doing unpleasant tasks. For example, maybe you've realized that your words get you in trouble because you instantly say whatever comes into your head. Or perhaps you put off studying because you don't like homework, or you'll think of any excuse not to clean your room. There are many ways in which we all neglect to practice discipline and self-control. And often we get discouraged when we realize we can't be disciplined all the time. But there's one very simple and very important way that you can begin to develop the character of a disciplined warrior. You can start with the little things.

Starting small can help you achieve some success quickly. Then that success can encourage you to keep going on the path of self-control. The key is not to try to do too much right away, but to choose one or two areas and then chip away at them. You may find that, with this approach, you recognize your progress in very short order. Do you need to go to bed half an hour earlier on school nights to ensure you get enough sleep? If you aren't ready to sacrifice a half-hour, what about heading to bed just 15 minutes earlier than usual? Do you tend to be late to class because you always stop at your locker for your English book? What if you just carried that one extra book to your previous class, so you wouldn't be delayed by the traffic around your locker?

4

Can you think of one or two small things that will help you practice self-control? Can you pause a little longer before you speak, or could you offer your friends another slice of pizza before you take one yourself? Will a deep breath help you see the big picture when your younger sister irritates you? Would you be willing to walk slowly to the school cafeteria rather than rush? What other little things can you try in order to build your self-control?

## Voice of a Warrior

*"Often, just a little bit of self-control can be the difference between being content and happy, and living your life feeling sour and resentful."*

—Nick, 14

**4**

## A Story from the Warrior's Path

Self-control can mean different things. It can mean restraining yourself from seizing an opportunity like the chance to eat the last piece of cake when no one is looking. Likely I'm in good company when I say that it's difficult. In other situations, self-control can mean not punching back when you're hit. Self-control shows how strong you can be—not when you *do* fight back, but when you could choose *not* to. To me, self-control means having the skills to defend yourself, but being able to determine when they should be used.

Self-control may come naturally to some people, but for others it takes practice. If the idea of "look before you leap" isn't in someone's nature, then that person has to work to become more conscious of what he or she is doing on impulse. For example, when you're insulted, a typical impulsive reaction would be to snap back with your own insult. The other choice would be to ignore the comment or walk away. That's a sign of self-control.

Impulse can often overtake self-control, despite Taekwondo's tenets or what we've been taught by our mothers. Once, despite my better judgment, I went against the principles I'd learned. Instead of walking away from a bully, I responded with a swift kick.

Consequences followed.

Afterward, all I could really think of was how I could show more self-control the next day. Not only that, but I would also show perseverance by not giving up on my goal of becoming more self-controlled.

—Sasha, 15

## Closing Thoughts on Self-Control

Warriors—people of positive thought and positive action—know that self-control is very difficult to achieve. But they also know that they can build themselves up so that they have confidence in their ability to say "yes" and "no" at the right times. As a warrior, have you noticed that you are often your own greatest enemy, as you struggle with urges and your desires to do things that aren't good for you? Can you see that this journey to achieve self-control is a lifelong journey? Take a first step—and don't expect perfection. Accept your mistakes when you make them, move on, and make a promise to yourself to do better next time. And always remember: be patient with yourself.

As you continue on your journey, you might also remind yourself that self-control is not about denying yourself all pleasures, or about making yourself miserable by forcing yourself to do (or not do) something. It's a way of thinking, a way of approaching the world. It's rooted in self-knowledge, thinking about and knowing what is good for you. If you develop the ability to see yourself clearly and determine what sorts of actions will help you reach your goals, then you'll find ways to take those actions. You'll also develop true independence, because you'll be taking responsibility for your own thinking and your own actions. Can you do something today to take the first step?

Great souls have will.
Feeble ones have only wishes.

Chinese proverb

## The Fifth Principle
# Indomitable Spirit

On the afternoon of the fifth day, the teacher led the students
to the center of town. They had all been to this spot many times
before. Four roads came together here, and it was always a busy
place. A wide array of merchants sold their wares at this intersec-
tion, and those townspeople who could afford to buy expensive
goods were fond of shopping here. On this day, there was as much
activity as ever. People went about the business of buying and selling, and moving from one place to another on the crowded streets.
The students watched the bustling scene—so different from their
quiet classroom on the mountain—in silence.

    Master Yi reached out his arms to his students and called
them together. They crowded around him as he spoke. "Do you
remember yesterday, how the birds moved in the trees and across
the sky? They came and went in an instant. They were always
flitting and darting, going about their business of being birds. Look
today at the people, too, going about the business of being people.
Some of them move quickly; others move calmly. Some of them
buy things; others sell them. This is life for many people, the buying and selling of things. And those who have money seem to love

the marketplace. But look closely. Do you see anyone here who is doing something different?"

The students looked at the crowd, trying to find someone who did not seem to fit in. Finally, one of the younger, newer students stepped forward. She was a slim girl with long hair. "Yes, there is an old woman," she said. "She is all bent over and looks very tired. But she is smiling. She is kissing all of the children when they come close to her."

Master Yi nodded and said, "Let her teach you this: In the midst of pain, there can be courage. The life of possessions is not always the life of having. To encourage others is to encourage yourself." He pressed his palms together and then intertwined his fingers. He continued, "To be true in this life is to be with hope. If you think the world is dark, then it will be dark. If you think the world is light, the sun will always shine. If you believe, then you will see."

He paused to watch the woman silently for a few moments, and the students did the same. Then Master Yi pointed at her, saying, "The woman's hands are always young as they reach toward others with kindness. Her kiss is like the kiss of a child, generous and innocent, hopeful and pure. If you try to live with a spirit that is dead, then you are dead. Let your heart be full, even when you feel you have nothing. The spirit of life is full of cheer. It will never be defeated—by pain or disappointment, by hopelessness or fear."

One of the older students frowned at this. He looked at Master Yi and then around at his companions. This boy was often recognized as an energetic leader and skillful writer. He said to the teacher, "But surely we cannot always be so cheerful. You said that our lives will be difficult. We must bear our load and move onward. We must grit our teeth and be determined."

Master Yi nodded as he replied, "Endurance does not mean misery. You will feel as good as you allow yourselves to feel. Find a benefit in everything. The light must come from within you. Let it shine on others, too."

He turned back to look at the woman, hunched over but smiling. She still moved among the children. Many of the little ones hugged her. Then Master Yi said:

Looking is good. Seeing is better. Listening is good.
Hearing is better. Hear this poem with your hearts:

You, too, have stepped away, your hands raised
as if to say, 'Enough. Enough.'
In the mirror, your face has shown the long lines
of neglect, your lips hanging like heavy leaves
in a garden gone bad.
Your yard is full of weeds.

What is it then that pulls us back,
allows us to look within and see the light?
In the end, it will be you, doing it for yourself,
unclenching your fist and opening your hands
to receive all good things.

You will hold in your stomach,
clear your head of every tired thought,
and step into the sun.

Master Yi fell quiet again and stood very still, as did the students. They continued listening to the sounds and absorbing the activity of the town. After a few moments, Master Yi turned and walked among the students, who parted to let him pass. Then they took one final look at the marketplace and followed their teacher. The road they had traveled to reach the town opened before them, and they walked together deliberately and thoughtfully, leaving the busy place behind them.

# Four Fundamentals for the Warrior

Master Yi wants his students to see that indomitable spirit, a positive attitude that can never be defeated, will help them succeed in their lives. It will bring them hope even when things go wrong. The Hwarangdo demonstrated indomitable spirit in battle whenever they faced an enemy that outnumbered them. Part of their code—never retreat in battle—reflected a confident and ferocious attitude. As a modern warrior, you can have the same optimistic spirit in your daily life. In fact, if you learn to approach every day with hope, you may find that you will be more cheerful— and more successful. Have you ever wondered if you can make your life as happy and as successful as you want it to be? These four fundamentals, if you practice them, will help you develop the indomitable spirit of the warrior:

- Learn to motivate yourself.
- Find a benefit in everything.
- Show enthusiasm.
- Step forward.

## Learn to Motivate Yourself

Do you sometimes want to "walk the easy road," to have someone hand you something even when you don't work for it? Do you occasionally want a high grade in a class, even when you don't study or put forth the necessary effort? If so, then you're like the rest of us! We all have periods when we feel lazy or unmotivated.

But all warriors know that they have to act and do. They know that they'll get results only when they commit themselves to putting forth their best effort—and then do so. And they know that they can't rely upon others to push them forward toward their goals. They must motivate themselves—even when it's difficult.

Have you ever had a teacher, coach, or other mentor who was a terrific motivator? If you've been around this sort of person, you know that he or she can inspire you to do just about anything—including work harder than you ever have before. This person might even have become a model for how you want to live your life. But even without such an example, you can still find ways to motivate yourself to work hard and not get discouraged. Three important tools will help you do this. The first tool is to have a clear goal. The second is visualizing yourself working toward that goal and achieving it. And the third is practicing positive self-talk.

Here's an example of these tools in action: Pete was a catcher on his school's baseball team. He was smaller than most catchers, and, although he was strong, he was not as muscular as some other players. But Pete practiced so hard every day that he almost made the other players look lazy, even when they were putting forth solid effort. One day when a fellow player asked Pete what motivated him, he answered, "I have to work hard because I'm going to go to the University of Southern California to play baseball."

It was brave of Pete to admit that he wanted to play at USC. The school has always had one of the best baseball programs in the country. Some of Pete's teammates thought he was a dreamer, but they never criticized him. He was an enthusiastic, natural leader, and his work ethic was unmatched. They often heard him talking to himself in practice and in games, saying things like, "See it, Pete. Visualize the ball taking off from your bat! That's the way to hit!" When Pete graduated from high school, he enrolled at USC, walked onto the baseball field, and won a spot on the team. He got a position as an outfielder, and although he never became a star, he proved how powerful self-motivation can be. He achieved a goal that others thought was impossible.

Do you think you can use Pete's example to motivate yourself? Take a look at how he operated. First, he had a goal. (It was a long-term goal, but he focused on the present, as well. He went to every practice with an enthusiastic, persevering spirit.) Second, he kept positive images of his success in his mind. And third, he practiced positive self-talk. He was a great example of hope and enthusiasm, and a master at motivating himself.

## Voice of a Warrior

"To me, indomitable spirit means that nobody can get you down. When someone tries to mess with your mind and tell you you're not good enough, they can't touch you because your self-confidence is too high."

—Asad, 15

Consider a situation in your life that requires you to motivate yourself. What if you have a difficult exam, and you want to get a higher grade than you've ever gotten in that class before? Maybe you want to get to know someone better, but you're not sure how to approach him or her. Or how about your personal interests? Do you want to invent something, perform a difficult dance routine, or write a great short story?

## Room for Reflection

- Who has really motivated you in your life? What qualities does this person have? Do you remember anything specific he or she has said that helped motivate you?

- Take some quiet time to imagine yourself succeeding at something you want to achieve. Try not to imagine only the endpoint of the success. Also develop some specific, positive images of steps you can take along the way toward that goal.

- What is one of your proudest accomplishments? What challenges or struggles did you overcome to reach this milestone, and how did you feel when you succeeded?

- Try to think of a powerful, positive statement that you can use to encourage yourself during rough times. Why will this statement help you? What does it mean to you?

Try to be specific with your goal. Then visualize working toward it and achieving it. And all along the way, engage in positive self-talk to keep yourself enthusiastic. If you can use all three of these tools every day, you'll find that you get better and better at motivating yourself. Then you can confidently and passionately take the necessary steps toward your success.

## Find a Benefit in Everything

*After being under siege for many years, the people in the small kingdom found it very difficult to remain optimistic. The warriors were weary from day after day of battle, children often went without food, and the king struggled to keep his people from falling into despair. One day the king called his leaders together and said, "We need an example for everyone to follow. We have been able to maintain our courage and our spirit for many, many years—but now our people badly need someone to inspire them. You warriors must think of someone who can step forward to be a model for the kingdom."*

*The next day the senior warriors brought a teenage boy before the king. One of the boy's hands hung limp and useless at his side.*

The king scoffed, saying, "Why did you bring me this boy? You are the finest warriors our kingdom has ever known, and you bring me an injured boy to inspire the people?"

The senior warrior replied, "My king, if you will listen to this young warrior, you will know why we brought him to you." So the king sat back and said to the boy, "Speak."

The boy said, "My king, I have heard that you think the people need encouragement, and that they feel defeated after all of these years. Well, they simply cannot yet see the benefit of their struggle. Two years ago, just after I was accepted to train with these great warriors, my strong hand was crushed beneath the wheel of a wagon. I cried for days after this accident—not only from the pain, but from the disappointment and fear that I might no longer be able to fulfill my dream of being a warrior. But then I realized that I needed only one hand to fight with a sword—and I still have my entire body to use as a weapon to defend our kingdom. So for eight hours a day, I practiced with the sword in what was once my weaker hand, until other people began to fear my skill. My skill might never have been so great had I never lost my good hand. I lost something that was important to me—but my heart and my skill are both stronger because of my loss. Now some of my companions believe that I may one day be the greatest warrior ever to serve you. Our people must see, too, that our struggles during this difficult time can help us grow in our resolve. We are learning not only to care for one another, but also to be resourceful and more fiercely determined. Things will not get better right away. But they will get better, if we can allow our hardship to strengthen us and not defeat us!"

The king smiled. "You are what the people need," he said. "You have seen a great benefit in a terrible loss. You have worked hard to overcome your setback—and that is exactly what our kingdom must do. We must realize that our circumstances can make us stronger—and that our endurance and determination are strengths. Tomorrow, young man, I will bring you before the people and give you a new horse—and I will announce that you will lead our great warriors into their next battle."

It's never easy to believe that a loss could benefit us. But that's what the young warrior in this story did. Real warriors see their setbacks as opportunities for growth. If they've put forth their best efforts and still not achieved their goals, they learn from their hardships and use their losses to spur them to train or to study harder. They do not complain. They learn to rebound from disappointment and courageously face their next challenge, having learned good lessons. And they know how to fuel the fire of their determination with an optimism that will never waver. As a warrior, you've surely experienced disappointments in your life—perhaps many. Some may have hurt you very deeply. But is there a way that these setbacks can actually motivate you?

**Voice of a Warrior**

*"There are two paths to take after you have been disappointed. You can become bitter, or you can learn. If you choose to learn, more doors will open up to you. I choose to keep learning and practicing."*

—Mikaela, 17

Naturally, your successes can help build your indomitable spirit, too, as they give you confidence. In fact, success is a great motivator. And we all have to be careful that our mistakes do not discourage us so much that we think less of ourselves as human beings. If you have a hard time finding a benefit in something that has happened, you might try to practice the motivational tools from the previous fundamental, especially imagining your success and practicing positive self-talk. Or you might make a list of some sad or discouraging experiences that you've been through. Then, next to each event you've listed, write down something you learned from that experience. Doing this may help you see that some of your hard times—even those that were very painful or disappointing—also benefited you in some way.

## Show Enthusiasm

Do you know someone who seems to be fearless and enthusiastic in nearly every situation? We often see heroism displayed in the movies and learn in the news of people performing extraordinary deeds. On the other hand, we tend to think of ourselves as regular folks who have little or no opportunity to show such spirit. But this may not be the case at all. People all around us show qualities of the warrior when they help someone even if they don't feel like it, when they support a person who is being harassed in school, or when they smile at a stranger. These actions have strong roots in a strong spirit. The warrior in you can shine when you don't withhold your positive feelings, but allow them to burst forth with enthusiasm. You may be more courageous than you think you are.

Andrea showed this sort of courage. She was a clarinetist in the school band. Even though she wasn't the school's most outstanding musician, she loved being in band. She had fun performing as a part of a group, and she especially enjoyed band practices, when she got to spend time with people who shared some of her interests.

It was already midyear when Taylor enrolled at the school and signed up for band, appearing on the first day after winter break and sitting as last chair in the clarinet section. After band practice that day, Andrea approached Taylor, smiled, and said, "I hope you like it here. We have a great time in band, and although the other sections don't agree with me, the clarinets are the best section in the band! See you tomorrow."

It took enthusiasm—and bravery—for Andrea to approach Taylor, smile, and extend a welcome like that. Perhaps Andrea just couldn't stifle her enthusiasm for band, or she was feeling especially happy and confident that day. Maybe she remembered being a new kid in school herself. Whatever the case, she shared her positive outlook with positive words.

How many people do you know who welcome new students or reach out to someone who seems alone? Why don't some people let their enthusiasm show, do you think? Can you think of opportunities when you could allow your enthusiasm to show in a way that focuses on someone else and attempts to spread positive spirit?

Consider what you know, what you're good at, and especially what you're passionate and enthusiastic about. Now think about ways you could bring others along on this experience, sharing your enthusiasm with them and perhaps reminding them that they, too, have much to give. Such an approach to other people is courageous. Do you think that such cheerful energy, such an enthusiastic spirit, might be contagious, too? How do you respond to those who encourage *you*? See if your positive energy will return to you and give you new drive and motivation.

It's not always easy to show enthusiasm. We all feel low sometimes. But warriors somehow find the spirit to motivate themselves—and then perhaps to motivate others. Here are three things you might try as you develop your indomitable spirit. The first is to compliment someone sincerely on something he or she did well. The second idea is to encourage someone to try something you think he or she might succeed at. Or, smile and say hello to a student at your school who seems lonely. See if these acts of indomitable spirit work for you, and reflect on how you feel when you try them.

True warriors try hard not to dwell on the negatives in their lives. Instead, they find things to be positive about—and then they reach out to others with that positive spirit. As a warrior, you don't need to look like a movie star or have the most fashionable clothes. All you need to do is recognize that the warrior spirit lies within you. Others will see it when you connect with them in a positive and enthusiastic way. Do you know someone right now who might benefit from your enthusiasm?

## Step Forward

If you've stepped up, shown enthusiasm, and given encouragement, you've already moved toward the next principle of indomitable spirit. Too often we avoid putting ourselves into situations because we're afraid that others will criticize us, or that we'll make mistakes that embarrass us. Fear is usually the major reason we avoid stepping forward. Maybe the best way to overcome fear is to face it head-on. Have you ever discovered that actually doing something isn't always the hardest part of a challenge? Often, we spend so much time and energy *thinking* about doing something that our fears become larger than they need to be. But sometimes just diving in—or stepping forward—is the best way to overcome your fears.

### Room for Reflection

- The English leader Winston Churchill said, "Success means going from failure to failure without the loss of enthusiasm." What do you think his words have to do with the principle of indomitable spirit?

- Who is a courageous person you know? In what ways does this person show courage?

- What activity or knowledge of yours makes you feel excited and energized? How might you share this enthusiasm and positive spirit with others?

DJ stepped forward in a brave way when he was a junior in high school. He'd always been shy, but he'd recently gained new confidence through his training in Taekwondo. He was friends with a group of guys who had gone to his grade school and middle school, but lately he'd started to drift apart from them. They were a tough bunch who were drawn to fighting and general troublemaking. DJ was beginning to think they didn't always use good judgment. But they were fun to hang out with, and he still liked them.

One day after gym class, five of the boys were roughing up a skinny freshman, having some "fun." The freshman was trying his best to escape, but the older guys surrounded him, raising his shirt over his head, laughing, and pushing him around. DJ walked into the locker room and stopped, wondering what to do. He felt bad for the freshman, but he'd been friends with these other boys for so long. DJ continued to hesitate for a moment. Then, squaring his shoulders and standing as tall as he could, he stepped inside the circle, grasped the freshman's elbow, and walked him out of the locker room, saying sternly, "Hurry up and get to class. Go on. Don't be late." Then DJ and the freshman walked to their separate classrooms. The older boys just stood there, surprised at what had happened.

DJ stepped forward in an uncomfortable situation. He knew that the older boys were bullying someone. Despite the fact that these guys were his longtime friends, DJ stepped in, in a confident, nonconfrontational way. Do you think he was at all afraid when he did this? How do you think the older boys saw DJ afterward? What would *you* do in such a situation?

Stepping forward often means taking a risk, whether big or small. You have chances to step forward each day. Maybe you have an opportunity to say something to comfort a friend. Maybe you know you'd benefit from staying after school and asking a teacher for extra help in social studies. Maybe you'd be in a safer environment if you stepped forward by stepping *away* from certain people you know.

How can you step forward at school, at home, or among your friends? Think about how you might prepare yourself to act out this fundamental of indomitable spirit with confidence.

## A Story from the Warrior's Path

The thought of autumn in high school always paints a uniquely nostalgic picture in my mind: the smell of the first chilly day, the colors of the changing leaves, the sound of a drumline cracking across the air by the lightof Friday night's home game. But the autumn of my first year of high school was not so idyllic. Instead, it was marked by tearful nights, and unsteady, frightening days. That was the autumn when my best friend was diagnosed with anorexia nervosa, a life-threatening eating disorder.

As the seriousness of my friend's condition became clear, I began to realize that, as much as she needed the support of others to help her through this struggle, I had always looked to her to strengthen my own spirit. The feeling of powerlessness to help someone you care deeply about is not only frightening, but lonely, as well. I felt as though my spirit would not be enough to give her the strength she had given me in better times. And it was then that I realized that my spirit did not exist solely within myself. It was something larger, something shared between people—among friends, in a family, or in a community. Indomitable spirit can be found in anyone because it exists within *everyone*. Even when our own strength seems to falter, we can find strength in those we care about and those who inspire us. When my friend was sick, I called on the times when she had strengthened my spirit with hers. Others who loved her did the same. Together we helped strengthen *her* indomitable spirit in a time of difficulty. As the seasons turned, our collective spirit grew, and the strength she found in herself and in others fueled our own, until the next autumn she once again stood among the crowd, watching our home team from the bleachers, the floodlights illuminating her face.

—Morgan, 16

## Closing Thoughts on Indomitable Spirit

As a warrior, you might find that indomitable spirit is very difficult to practice. Distractions and temptations can often keep us from being positive and courageous. You might try to develop a strong spirit by first taking small steps—doing something that may seem insignificant but still challenges you. When you face fear, difficulty, or discouragement, you may be inspired by Pete's positive images of success, the young warrior's injured hand, Andrea's enthusiasm, and DJ's step forward. All of these people found ways to enter the world of the warrior, even though they faced obstacles outside or inside themselves.

We all get tired and discouraged at times, and we can't always practice indomitable spirit with intensity. Sometimes stress gets to us, and we may be negative occasionally, even if we usually do a pretty good job of staying enthusiastic and positive. When that happens, perhaps you'll benefit from taking some time by yourself, resting, and recollecting a few of Master Yi's words to his students:

> "To encourage others is to encourage yourself."
> "If you believe, then you will see."
> "Let your heart be full, even when you feel you have nothing."
> "The spirit of life is full of cheer."
> "The light must come from within you. Let it shine on others, too."

Do you find any inspiration in these words? Maybe you could memorize one of these statements to encourage you to practice indomitable spirit when you find it hard to do so. Or maybe there are other sayings that have great meaning for you. What are the words that help *you* stay motivated and enthusiastic?

He who wishes to secure the good of others has already secured his own.

Confucius

# The Sixth Principle
# Community Service

The next day, Master Yi took his students into town again. This time he did not stop at the familiar spot where people gathered to engage in business. Instead, he led the student-warriors down a narrow street toward the neighborhood where the poorest people lived. They passed dirty children and barking dogs, blind men and begging women. They stepped over dead animals and garbage. The street ended at the entrance to a stone building, the prison for the worst criminals. The teacher knocked at the huge door, and the doorkeeper opened without saying a word. The teacher then led the pupils into a dirty courtyard, the center of the prison, where criminals in their cells surrounded them. Some of the prisoners laughed, some shouted, and some simply stared in silence at the young people.

Master Yi began, "The only evil in the world is the confusion and ignorance of the human heart. Before you crush evil, know that you crush yourself as well. In violence, there is always defeat and sadness. Since there is no victor in violence, you must love your enemy."

He could see that some of his students were very uncomfortable in the setting. But he did nothing to relieve their uneasiness. He went on, "Remember that you are as guilty as the thief. The sun shines on both of your heads, and the rain falls on his roof, too. The air that he breathes out, you breathe in. His poverty and your wealth are intertwined. His violence is rooted in his pain."

One of the young people—a boy with an expression of both discomfort and annoyance on his face—spoke up. "We did not put these people here. We did not make them commit their crimes or force them to make the choices that brought them to this place. Why did you bring us here, Teacher? Are we supposed to feel guilty, when they are the guilty ones?"

Master Yi's eyes remained soft as he replied, "Just as in integrity you connect yourself to yourself, now you must know how you connect to others. To acknowledge the connectedness of all people is a sign of wisdom. All of you, too, stand in these cells, your hands idle and your heads hanging low. You, too, ache for freedom and joy."

A young, spirited girl spoke up. "But Master Yi, we feel joyful most days. Here in prison it is hard to feel the joy of freedom."

"Yes, it is," replied Master Yi. "But it is important that you try to see with the eyes of those in pain. When you reach out to help a stranger, you reach out to yourself as well."

*Motioning for the pupils to gather very closely around him, Master Yi said:*

Looking is good. Seeing is better. Listening is good. Hearing is better. Hear this poem with your hearts:

Let us walk, all of us, into the wide light
of the pasture.
We will join our hands as we move,
believing in our own airy lives,
together, at last,
the young and the old,
the fast and the slow,
the bound and the free.

The trees behind us will be in bloom,
and the sounds of spring will follow
the narrow sleeve of day,
and the trials of this season.

We will smile and we will speak
the words that we all understand.

*The students looked around after Master Yi had finished speaking. The prisoners continued to stare at the young people. Finally, Master Yi motioned his pupils out of the courtyard and back toward the entrance to the stone prison. The doorkeeper slowly opened the thick, heavy door, and the students and their teacher walked out into the narrow streets of the town.*

## Community Service

# Four Fundamentals for the Warrior

The teacher hopes that his students will embrace community service. He wants them to see that all people basically have the same needs. We are all part of the human family, and that means that we are all responsible for helping others. Warriors have always served someone other than themselves. They are ready to sacrifice their time, their energy, and their lives. As a modern warrior, you have the power to open your heart to others who need assistance. You have youth and energy, discipline and strength. You may already be starting to understand how to reach out to others in a spirit of community. But it can take time to fully embrace this principle. If you're not quite there yet, these four fundamentals can help you grow:

- See the "Big I."
- Realize your worth—and that of others.
- Seek humility.
- Give without expecting to get.

## See the "Big I"

The term "Big I" refers to seeing our place in the human community, and embracing our duty to share our time and our talents with other members of that community. Those who focus on the "Little I" tend to look out only for themselves in a narrow way. But the Big I is much more than the individual self. If we understand the Big I, we take responsibility for the well-being of the community. Warriors accept their responsibility to be of service so that they can make the world a more peaceful one. They reach out to other people and try to help them lead more fulfilling lives.

Another aspect of the Big I is accepting others without regard to their looks, status, abilities, disabilities, successes, or failures. The world of the Big I is a place where we recognize our connection to others and we act on that connection.

Naturally, the transition to the Big I can take time. We have to look beyond our individual goals and accomplishments, our specific troubles and challenges, and reach out to others. We must learn to grow beyond our small, individual selves and reach beyond the world of arrogance and isolation.

Maybe you've heard the story of Roberto Clemente, the first Latin American baseball player to enter the Hall of Fame. Born in Puerto Rico, Clemente was a star on the field. But he's considered a hero because of what he did off the field. On New Year's Eve, 1972, he was on a plane bound for Nicaragua, where he was going to help deliver aid to the victims of an earthquake. But Clemente never got to Nicaragua. His plane went down in the ocean. His body was never found, but the story of his sacrifice lives on.

You may also know about Clara Barton, who is credited with founding the American Red Cross. Even as a girl, Barton felt the need to tend to others. When her brother was seriously ill, she cared for him, and then she became a teacher while she was still a teenager. Her best-known acts of community service took place during the American Civil War. Barton tended to wounded soldiers on the war's battlefields, often putting her own life in danger as she provided aid and comfort.

One story you won't have heard is about a teen named Alex. Every day after school, he took the bus to his grandparents' house so he could read to his grandfather, do some household chores, and help his grandmother prepare dinner.

Alex had realized that as his grandparents aged, they would need more help with their daily activities. So he stepped forward to offer them his time, love, and care.

Alex isn't famous, but there are thousands of stories like his. Perhaps you see yourself as just a regular person. You may not believe that you could have the profound influence of Roberto Clemente or Clara Barton. But the truth is that you can still embrace the Big I, just as Alex did. The important thing to remember is that warriors do not live only for themselves. They serve. They believe in the Big I and they act with concern, conviction, and courage. Have you thought of how you might connect with others in small but powerful ways? Can you commit some of your time and your energy to an individual or a group of people who could benefit from your help? Maybe you know of an elderly neighbor who needs someone to shop for her groceries each week or mow her yard. Maybe you know a child who is having trouble reading, and you can help him after school. Or maybe you want to visit a nursing home for an hour on Saturdays and play bingo with the residents. The action doesn't need to be a huge one. How do you think you might feel if you serve or help someone else without being asked to do so?

## Voice of a Warrior

*"Some people are very down because they can't stop looking at themselves. They can't get past themselves and care for others."*

—Blake, 15

## Realize Your Worth—and That of Others

*One year the Won Hwa asked some of the Hwarangdo to compose poems to celebrate the wedding of the king's daughter. Each student would get an opportunity to read his or her poem during the wedding reception. One of the young warriors selected was not known as an especially good poet. He was most admired for his skills on horseback. He always felt more comfortable when he was on horseback, removed from close contact with other people. Part of the reason for this was that he had a birthmark on his right cheek, which caused him to feel self-conscious and shy around people.*

*Three days before the wedding reception, one of the Won Hwa found out that this boy had not yet written a poem. When she asked him why, he sighed and answered, "I am no good at writing poetry. I am only good on a horse. You should not have selected me. The other students are better poets than I am—and they are much more attractive, too. Let me serve the king in other ways, please."*

*The Won Hwa sat down with the boy and said, "If you wish to be a better poet, you must practice. I believe this experience will help you improve as a writer. And I am sure your poem will be just fine. I will even help you with it, if you like. And remember that your worth is not in your appearance, or even in your skill alone. Think of it this way:*

### Room for Reflection

- Can you recall any times when you felt especially connected with other people—your family, friends, classmates, or others? How would you describe that feeling? What caused that sense of connection?

- Do you know anyone who seems to embody the idea of the Big I? How does he or she show this fundamental in action? What special attitude does this person have about life, in general?

- What personal qualities of yours tend to worry or bother you? Do you feel you should change or accept those qualities?

- How do you think others tend to judge you? Do you judge yourself by those same factors?

*Do you think less of your fellow students if they do not ride a horse as well as you do, or if they appear awkward on horseback?"*

*"Of course not," said the boy. "I don't see them only as people who can or cannot ride a horse well."*

*"How do you see them?" asked the Won Hwa.*

*"I see them as people, young people like me," he said. "That's all. Just people who are trying to do their best."*

*"And so what makes your situation any different? You are able to recognize others' worth as human beings, regardless of their talents or their physical features. Everyone sees you the same way. Now you must see your own worth, not as a horseman, but as a human being."*

Does this story remind you of yourself, or of someone you know? How often do you—like the warrior in the story—judge your own worth based upon your appearance, your popularity, or your ability to succeed at something? Maybe sometimes you find it hard to see your own worth because others have criticized you, or because society tells us that we should appear a certain way.

Similarly, it's easy to look at other people and judge them by how many friends they have, how much money they make, or where they live. And we naturally worry that others are judging us based on those same external factors. Don't we sometimes look at ourselves and think we should be better looking or have nicer clothes? While our culture may encourage us to value what people see on the outside, a warrior sees what is on the inside, too—*especially* what is on the inside.

Understanding that all of us are alike in our humanity allows us not to be alone. We're all imperfect. When we're discouraged or sad, we often need others to remind us of our true value—not what we've done or failed to do, but our value as human beings with gifts and defects. Likewise, we can be aware that others have the same needs as we do,

among them the need for companionship and a sense
of belonging.

You might rethink the idea of what it means to have
worth. Consider the times when you worry about how you
look, what you wear, or what you have accomplished or not
accomplished. Do you think that sometimes you're too hard
on yourself? Are there also times when you're too critical of
others, and fail to recognize their true worth?

## Seek Humility

Once we see that we're part of the human family and that
we all have similar needs, hopes, and desires, we may understand more about the Big I and the essential worth all of us
possess. When this philosophy of the warrior is part of our
lives, we become people of greater action—positive action.

This next fundamental might be tricky to grasp at first.
It's human nature to want to be recognized and appreciated.
One of the basic temptations we all face is to raise ourselves
up, sometimes at others' expense, in order to make ourselves
feel superior. But this is not the way of the warrior. How
do you feel when you are insulted? Have you ever insulted
someone else to make that person feel inferior and to try to
raise your own feeling of worth? Consider how our culture
seems to value the "winner" and scorn or toss aside the
"loser." Plenty of common expressions play into this notion:
"No one likes a loser" and "Be a winner" and "Second place
isn't good enough." Of course, competition can be healthy
at times. It can motivate us to work hard and achieve big
things. But the notion of seeking humility and striving to
serve others is at the center of the warrior's heart.

To seek humility begins with the attitude that you aren't
inherently superior to anyone else—and, by the same token,
no one else is inherently superior to you. Furthermore, warriors recognize that they aren't above doing any task, as long

as someone doesn't force them to do something that would degrade them or make them feel ashamed.

One respected martial arts master always encouraged his highest-ranking, black-belt students to vacuum the floor, sweep the entrance, and clean the bathrooms before they began their daily training. The teacher's message about humbling oneself was clear. The fact that the black belts did these chores showed that even the most advanced students weren't above any job, or superior to anyone else. Yes, they lined up in front of the lower-ranking students during class. But they also demonstrated humility by doing the cleaning and by helping their fellow students with their techniques.

A wealthy and powerful businessman who once enrolled in this teacher's school left after only one week. Was the training too hard? Was it boring? No. The businessman left because he refused to perform the customary bow, even though he knew that the teacher and the highest-ranking students would return the bow. He thought that his wealth and his status in the community placed him above the other students, even though he was a beginner in the martial arts. He was unwilling to humble himself.

## Voice of a Warrior

*"Once I started to look at how similar I am to other people, rather than how different, I was much happier. By seeing our similarities, I realized I am really worth something. I become part of a community—not an outcast."*

—Natalie, 16

To seek humility as a warrior is an act of love and care. It's a conscious act meant to reach out in a genuine and heartfelt manner, and to demonstrate and reinforce your unity with other people.

Are there times in your day when you can practice seeking humility? Maybe you could take care to clean up your spot at the school cafeteria, or pick up a piece of litter at the bus stop. Can you clean the dishes at home without being asked, or let someone go ahead of you in line at a store? You might even strive to be humble on a larger scale. Do you think you can seek humility by giving away some of your money or an object you value? Another way to practice this fundamental is by teaching others a skill that you possess. Keep in mind that all of community service is rooted in humility. What are ways that you can practice this humility at school, at home, and among your friends? How about in the wider community?

## Give Without Expecting to Get

Many times when we give something (including our time and energy), we hope to receive something in return. It's true that as we give honestly, our warrior's heart should grow, but how about if we expect *nothing* in return? Is it possible that we can honestly be devoted just to giving— and not be concerned with any payback?

This fundamental is at the heart of community service. While it's pretty easy to give to others when we receive something in return, it can be much harder to find it in our hearts to look only at the ones we are serving. You're already working on strengthening yourself and your warrior's heart with the principles of courtesy, integrity, perseverance, self-control, and indomitable spirit. Now can you embrace the principle in which the warrior loses the self? And can you see that if you lose yourself you may actually discover yourself?

In order to understand this fundamental more fully, think about the times when you feel most at peace with yourself and your place in the world. When do you feel free of stress and anxiety? When have you felt capable of accomplishing an important task? If you can recollect this peaceful yet powerful feeling, or put yourself in an environment where peace and confidence coexist, then you can tap into your ability to give away what you have and not feel depleted. You may discover that you can share your energy or your enthusiasm or a few kind words, without worrying about getting anything back. You just feel powerful enough to give, and you know that your gift will be important to someone else.

From this place of peace and power, try to take steps toward giving without expecting to get. You might merely say, "Nice job!" to someone who has earned a high grade in school. You might call a food shelf and offer to sort supplies on the weekend. You could pull your neighbor's emptied trashcans from the curb back to her garage, or offer to help your dad as he struggles to carry in the groceries. These sorts of efforts cost nothing more than your time—sometimes no more than a moment!—and yet, in making them, you'll be practicing an important fundamental of the warrior. You will not be giving out of fear or

## Room for Reflection

- What do you think Master Yi means when he says, "When you reach out to help a stranger, you reach out to yourself as well"? To which of the fundamentals of community service might these words best apply?

- When in your life are you apt to find it very difficult to seek humility? Can you think of any way that you can help yourself practice that fundamental?

- What do you think your greatest personal gifts or talents are? Are there ways you can share them with others? How might you give and feel as though you have not been depleted?

expectation. You'll be giving out of your true and strong self. And the remarkable truth you may discover is that you will not be depleted. In fact, giving from strength increases one's strength.

In real giving there is no selfishness, no expectation, and no worry. How do you think life would be if all of us could give—just a little bit—in this way?

There are many ways to give, but today you can try even another way of giving without expecting to get: work on giving of yourself by being attentive to people. Try to connect with others by showing a real interest in them. Ask questions about how they are doing at school or work, and about what they really like to do. See if they'll talk about themselves. Work at being patient and attentive, without forming judgments or giving opinions. Can you really hear them?

## A Story from the Warrior's Path

Early in my Taekwondo training, I remember thinking of the community service principle as a type of task to be completed on occasion. I participated in volunteer trips around town, adopting the common but restricted idea of community as a physical area. My understanding of community service grew as I expanded my understanding of a community. I started focusing on the value of human connection, on that feeling that comes from helping someone who needs it, and on the appreciation I had for all those who had been there for me when I needed it. I began understanding community as human connections expressed through kindness, however big or small. As a result, I became much more in touch with the situations of others around me, aware of disadvantages certain groups face and the role I could have in helping them find empowerment and fulfillment. I began participating in more long-term service groups, trying to integrate community service more permanently into my life, just as I tried to do with the other principles.

Now I understand community service as an *attitude*, a lifelong process rather than an occasional activity to check off a to-do list. To me it is the culmination and aim of the other principles: to craft yourself into a courteous and strong spirit not for the sake of being the best, but for the sake of using your skills to help others as you've been helped along the path. And it's not about the hours, or the location, or even the activity itself, really. It's about the people you connect with. It's about extending your sense of community by offering your hand to those you otherwise might not have even met.

—Terrell, 19

## Closing Thoughts on Community Service

In order to see that community service is truly part of the warrior's heart, we only have to remember that the lives of all warriors—including the Hwarangdo, the Japanese samurai, the medieval knights, and others—centered on their service to their leaders and to the people of their towns and countries. They served a cause greater than themselves, and they believed that their training was meant not to elevate themselves, but to give them the strength to serve.

Think of yourself as a warrior in daily life. Warriors' lives aren't always made up of huge undertakings, monumental victories, or dramatic struggles. Instead, they're usually comprised of conscious decisions, small sacrifices, and honest effort. The principle of community service allows you another way not only to strengthen your warrior's heart but also to contribute to a world that needs your help. You are as important to this world as any other human being, and any time you help others, you help make the world better. As a warrior, you have talent, energy, and conscience. Think about your abilities and strengths. How can *you* make a positive contribution to the world around you?

Music in the soul can be
heard by the universe.

Chinese proverb

# The Seventh Principle
# Love

On the morning of the seventh day, the students did not see their teacher at the quiet birch tree grove. At noon, he was not by the babbling stream. They looked for him in all of his favorite places, but could not find him. They began to grow worried.

Finally, in the middle of the afternoon, Master Yi found the young people sitting in his garden. They were talking about the last six days and wondering aloud if they would see him again. He laughed and said, "I told you that in one week I would leave you, but this is the seventh day, and the week is not yet over. Come. Let us take one more walk together, to where the water meets the land."

The student-warriors followed their old teacher on the long walk to the shore. They traveled over two hills and crossed a meadow. By the time they arrived, the sun was low in the sky. Master Yi motioned for his pupils to sit. They all faced the ocean and watched the sun sink toward the horizon.

The teacher began, "Look at the water—how the waves advance, how they retreat. They come and they go, just as this day has done, just as every day always has done and always will do. The waves are relentless as they touch the land. They reach it and wash over it, soaking into the sand without ceasing. The water and the earth always touch."

114

The students studied the movement of the waves, mesmerized by the peaceful rhythm.

Master Yi continued, "There is no end to the waves. And beneath your bodies, where you sit, you feel the sand, a million grains joined by their touching and your touching. Although you do not see every grain of sand, as you are connected to one, you are connected to all."

He fell silent and nodded his head slowly and deliberately. "Yes, so it is with all of you," he continued. "You love one another, but you must also love those you do not know and those you do not see, those you believe you should hate and those you believe you must scorn. Your love must touch everyone."

Some of the students nodded, as if they understood. Others appeared puzzled. After a moment, one of the younger students, a tall, muscular boy with a strong, square jaw, stood up and asked, "We have been training as fighters, too. How can we love everyone if we will one day need to fight?"

Master Yi continued, "That is the tragedy of war. You must hope you never have to fight. When one dies by the sword, we all die by the sword. The one who kills another, with sword or word, kills himself first and last."

Closing his eyes and shaking his head, Master Yi continued, "The one who enjoys fighting understands nothing of life. He does not know that success and achievement, victory and defeat, are as brief as the day. He does not know that love is the source of life."

Master Yi motioned for the student-warriors to stand and come close to him. As dusk settled on the group, he smiled and moved among his students, touching each of them on the shoulder, one by one. Then he said, "Remember that the inner master only reveals himself when the outer master withdraws. I must leave you now."

As the twilight deepened, the student-warriors' faces were very sad. The young people truly saw now that their teacher, whom they loved deeply, was indeed going to leave them. A tall, slender girl began to cry softly. A strong swordsman hung his head. The eldest of the group, an experienced leader named Yang, simply closed his eyes as a tear trickled down his face.

Master Yi was quiet for some time before he finally spoke again:

Looking is good. Seeing is better. Listening is good. Hearing is better. Hear this poem with your hearts:

Even in the approaching night,
we see,
our hearts open
to the gulls coming home to shore, bellying
over the breaking waves, floating
on the wordless wind, free of thought.

Quiet now,
we find ourselves in this life
playing the silent music of truth,
giving away what we have always had.

Desire is wanting.
No desire is having.
With love, we have.
With love, we are.

After he had spoken the last word, the master looked a few more moments at his students and smiled. His eyes were full of love. Then he turned and walked away from the water, toward the pasture, and into the open hand of the night. It was the last time his students ever saw him.

# Four Fundamentals for the Warrior

The teacher's words about love echo very strongly with the students. Their relationship with him and with one another is based upon a strong love. Yet he challenges them also to remember their relationship to everyone in the world. He reminds them that they are connected to every human being.

The love Master Yi talks about is different from the sort of love you may be thinking of. This isn't romantic love, and it isn't the feeling of love that we have for family and friends. Instead, the teacher suggests that love is a choice, a decision. This is love in the broadest and most challenging sense.

As a warrior, you may see that your actions are not merely deeds without meaning. They can be deeds that are rooted in the decision to love others as you love yourself. You can see now that the last two principles of community service and love are bound together very tightly. The fruit of love is service. And how much we do for others matters less than how much love we put into the action. Here are four fundamentals to help you develop the love and the heart of the warrior:

- Open up.
- Stop judging.
- Forgive others.
- Forgive yourself.

## Open Up

Imagine that you've been asked to babysit for a couple with three children under the age of seven. You have some experience babysitting. In fact, you really like kids. But the thought of being outnumbered three to one still worries you a bit. Before going to the job, you ask people for advice. Some say, "Be sure they know who is in charge!" Others tell you, "Don't let them take advantage of you." You even read some magazine articles that discuss techniques for dealing with unruly children. By the time you reach the babysitting job, you feel prepared. You're ready to handle any crisis.

The evening ends up going pretty well. At one point you have to give the five-year-old a "time out," and you have some trouble getting the kids to go to bed. But the parents seem pleased with your work, the children appeared to like you, and you liked them. In fact, the parents ask you to babysit the next weekend, too. The only problem is that you really didn't enjoy yourself. Being so focused, determined, and intense gave you a headache—and you're not sure you want to tackle the job again. In your heart, something just felt wrong. What do you think could be the problem?

Have you ever felt very frustrated in a similar situation, even though everything seems to go well? Does your heart sometimes feel uneasy, without any clear reason?

The "open up" fundamental deals with the feelings of frustration all of us have sometimes in our relationships with others. We are often preoccupied with methods of getting along with others or ways that we can "make things work" in our relationships. But when we can't relax our minds enough to simply enjoy the relationships, we end up fighting ourselves. We resist the opportunity for true interaction. Maybe we're trying *too* hard. Or perhaps we're more concerned with what we're doing than whom we're with.

Whatever the reasons, it's all too easy to become guarded and closed off rather than open and receptive. The warrior must guard against this closing down, and focus on opening up. It's often when we just relax and openly enjoy the company of others, especially those we love, that we receive the most energy and motivation.

The principle of community service is all about the action of giving. It's about serving others with our gifts, our time, and our material possessions. But love is about more than giving; it's about receiving, too. And this fundamental of opening up is a different sort of action. It's almost a purposeful inaction, as you simply let yourself receive the energy and the spirit of other people.

This idea might seem a bit strange to you at first. As a warrior, you're becoming a person of action. Yet, while the positive action of community service is the fruit of love, we all need to be careful not to do things for the sake of action alone. We want to invest our actions with meaning.

Voice of a Warrior

"Love is not just about those whose company you enjoy a lot. Love is about respecting the emotions and struggles of others, even if you don't know them or you even dislike them."

—Alejandro, 16

The next time you're around other people, try to be really aware of what they're saying and doing. Let yourself open up to the situation and to the words and actions of others. As you do so, you may become more aware of the potential for true interaction, in which you are engaged with and perhaps really understand someone else. Can you hear the underlying feelings that others are communicating? Do you find that this sort of opening up helps you feel more joined to others and to the world?

## Stop Judging

*During a particularly bad decade in the kingdom, the Hwarangdo had to go to battle nearly every year. Their enemy in a large neighboring territory was relentless in trying to take over the smaller kingdom, and the warriors felt as if they were on the verge of battle at every moment. The scouts reported the enemy's aggressive movements frequently, and the young warriors felt fatigued and stressed by the constant threat of invasion. One day, in the terrible heat of summer, the commanding warriors ordered the group to gather their belongings and get ready to leave immediately to support fellow warriors who were defending a mountain pass.*

*Complaining and negative thinking were never encouraged among the warriors. But at this stressful time, under these difficult conditions, grumbling began. One warrior, while bent over and tightening the straps of his sandals, did not see his superior approach. As he adjusted his sandals, he said to a few warriors nearby, "These other soldiers who want to fight us must not have minds of their own. Their kingdom is a mess, and their king is crazy. Can't they see that we will defeat them again and again? Don't they know that to follow a lunatic king like theirs is a sign of stupidity? Really, they must be so dimwitted that their mothers even find it hard to love them!"*

*Standing over the talkative warrior, the leader said sternly, "Stand up. You are here hugging your own high opinion of yourself. Think about it. Are you better than the one you may battle today?*

*How? You bent over to tighten your sandals, just as your enemy did. You slept on the ground last night, just as he did. You are obeying orders, just as he is doing. Today, if you face him in battle, the sun will shine on you both, will it not? And won't you breathe the same air? Each of you will hope to live. When you have drawn your sword, look into his eyes. You will see yourself."*

The superior reminds the young warrior that in many ways all of us are similar. As a young warrior yourself, you may have noticed that when you observe similarities in people, not just differences, your world opens up. You feel less alone, and you see more opportunity for happy relationships.

Naturally, though, we tend to notice our differences, too. We see that people have different strengths and weaknesses, different talents, different appearances, different personalities. Sometimes these differences are very noticeable, and we may judge people because of them. Or we can become preoccupied with ways we're different from others. For example, maybe you're especially self-conscious about your complexion, your clothing, your grades, or your body. The pressure to look for differences is sometimes very powerful.

## Room for Reflection

- Try to think of times in your day when you can listen to a friend without offering any judgment. How does it feel to do this?

- Who are the people in your life who seem to need special encouragement? What can you do to help them feel more positive?

- When do you find yourself feeling defensive and closing yourself off to others? How can you resist this tendency, and open up instead?

It's also easy to look at our differences as deficiencies. You might hear someone say, "Look at her. She looks so silly when she dances." Or "What's wrong with him? He can't even do the simplest writing assignment." Before we know it, we're hard at work labeling and calling out the deficiencies of others—highlighting our differences. But have you ever looked at your *own* deficiencies more closely?

It might sound backward at first, but the realization that all of us are lacking in some ways is a positive and powerful one. It can help us learn to embrace love for the great principle it is. By recognizing our own flaws, errors, and imperfections, we can start to tear down the barriers of prejudice, hatred, and indifference. Once we recognize and accept our own personal flaws, we might find it easier to stop judging or criticizing others for theirs. This doesn't mean that we should support poor behaviors by others. It simply means that we must accept the truth that we're all flawed. Do you think you can help build a more peaceful world, little by little, by not making harmful judgments?

Judging, criticizing, or condemning another person is not positive action. But understanding that we all make mistakes can be the root of positive action. Our minds make judgments all day long, every day. Even when we first see someone, we might think, "That dress looks bad on her." Or "That guy is always causing trouble." Or "He looks ridiculous in gym class." These judgments seem to come so quickly that, often, we don't even notice that we're judging. And naturally, then we wonder what people are thinking of us, what judgments they are making about our appearance or our abilities. While our minds may seem to run away with us at times, try to be aware today of how you *respond* to your own thoughts, judgments, and reactions. Take positive action by speaking up when you have something good to say about someone else—and by avoiding taking part in gossip. Work at letting go of judgments and at resisting the urge to criticize someone else. And if you see someone who needs encouragement or acceptance, offer it to them.

## Forgive Others

We already know that the warrior's heart is not centered on warfare. It is centered on self-improvement and service. True warriors focus on living productive lives and offering help and healing when they can. However, when others have injured us, we usually find it difficult to be healed. Our suffering can cause us to be angry and resentful. When we hang on to resentment, we live again and again in the past. We cling to it, reliving the hurt and the anger, and we allow the bitterness to grow—which only causes us to feel isolated and imprisoned. The only way to get rid of this isolation, this feeling of resentment, is through forgiveness. As hard as it is, this forgiveness frees us from our own pain. But it's often very hard to forgive.

You've probably faced many situations where forgiveness is possible but difficult. Perhaps within your family there are wounds that are hard to heal. Perhaps among your friends you've noticed resentment over wrongs or hurt feelings. Sometimes forgiveness is especially hard when people we care deeply about have caused us pain.

Maria had to cope with such a situation. Maria was a dedicated and successful student. She spent long hours studying for quizzes and tests, and she also volunteered to tutor others after school. While she did well in many of her classes, she was especially successful in her favorite classes, math and science.

A few days after a math test, Maria's teacher asked her to remain after class. He asked her to sit down and then he said, "Maria, you've always done very well in math. But on this exam, one of your classmates told me that you cheated. Your score was very good, but the student said she saw you working from our study guide, which you held under your desk."

Maria was shocked. She hadn't cheated, and she explained to her teacher that she would never do such a thing. She couldn't believe someone had falsely reported her to the teacher when she'd always been honest in her schoolwork. The teacher accepted her explanation, largely because of Maria's record. But Maria knew that her reputation had been damaged—and someone else had damaged it on purpose.

Maria's pain would not go away. She couldn't stop thinking about who had done this to her—and why. Eventually she found out through other students that someone she had helped study for the test, a very competitive student, was the one who had lied to the teacher. Maria was more hurt than ever. She'd always thought of this girl as her friend.

After a few days, she worked up the nerve to confront the girl and ask her if she'd made the false report to the teacher. At first the girl denied it, but finally she broke down in tears and confessed. "Yes. I told the teacher, and I know I should never have lied. I'm sorry."

**Voice of a Warrior**

*"I think that in today's society love is a misused word. Many people say that they 'love' something when all they do is like it. I feel that love has its own meaning for each person, but that if you truly love something you would give up everything you have for that one person or thing."*

—Mei, 13

The Seventh Principle: Love   125

"But why?" asked Maria. "Why would you attack me this way?"

"I envied your success," the girl replied. "For a while, I wanted to ruin you. Please forgive me. I'll tell Mr. Rath that I told the lie."

Maria was still very upset. She said, "Telling Mr. Rath will help him see the truth, but what about the stories people tell about me now in school? You can never stop those. You started the ball rolling."

Maria was right—rumors and exaggerated stories make their way around groups of people very quickly. Sometimes the real truth never even comes out at all. What could Maria do? Her pain wasn't going to fade right away just because the girl had apologized. Would Maria be angry at the other girl forever? Would she try to retaliate? What would *you* do?

It's easy to carry a grudge when someone wrongs us. Maybe you've rejected others because of their selfishness or thoughtlessness—or perhaps people you know have accused you of doing something you didn't do. As you build your warrior's heart, this fundamental of forgiving others may be one of the most difficult to practice. We don't always know how we'll respond to someone who hurts us or hurts people we care about. But remember that the true warrior tries to think and act as positively as possible, as often as possible. Warriors stay committed to the ideal of building a peaceful world—and a peaceful world can only come about through understanding and love. Is it possible to understand why someone has hurt you? Try to remember that often others bring us pain because of their natural, human weaknesses. And we hurt others because of our own weaknesses. Knowing this may not ease our pain, but it can help us make sense of it.

As with any ideal, talking about, writing about, or thinking about forgiving others is a lot easier than doing it. The healing process is hard, and the freedom of forgiving is difficult to achieve. The warrior has to surrender feelings of anger and resentment in order not to be imprisoned by them. To make a positive step in freeing yourself, think of a recent time when someone hurt you. Maybe someone criticized you or spread a false rumor about you. You have every right to be upset by such an incident—but if you can, try also to see that the other person's action was done out of weakness. Positive actions are done out of strength; negative ones are not. Knowing that someone hurt you because of a weakness such as fear or insecurity—and knowing, too, that you have weaknesses of your own—can you see a way to let go of resentment and remove the chains of living in the past? If you can forgive others in this way, you'll feel freer and happier—and you'll be one step farther along on the warrior's path.

## Forgive Yourself

Like the fundamental "forgive others," the fundamental "forgive yourself" demands that we let go of the painful past. This can be hard to do. When you don't meet your own expectations, are you filled with regret and remorse? Do you find it hard to get over your own mistakes and move ahead? What if you violate one of your values or ideals? As warriors, we hope and strive to always do the right thing. This can make forgiving ourselves extra difficult.

Think about some of your most prized values. What are they? Honesty? Loyalty? Kindness? Maybe you truly believe that people should show courtesy to others in all situations, even when it's difficult, and you do your best to uphold this value. You greet people kindly, including those whom others often ridicule. You've made every attempt to show respect for your elders. But then you have a bad day. Let's say you yell at your best friend for no apparent reason—or you shove him or her in frustration. Will you be able to apologize, accept your mistake, and move on? Or will you feel guilty and upset with yourself for days?

Here's another scenario. Imagine that you feel great pressure to succeed in a certain class at school, and there's an important homework assignment due tomorrow. But you also have to study for three other tests, you have your brother's birthday party to help plan, and you have play practice until 7 p.m. What will you do? You realize that one of your friends will give you the homework answers, but you don't want to take the shortcut. You know you'll need to know the material for the final exam anyway. And more than that, you have always thought that your integrity was more important than a grade on an assignment or a test. But in the end, you accept your friend's answers and turn in the homework for a good grade.

Situations like these aren't out of the ordinary. They can happen to anyone. In the first scenario, your action is spontaneous. In the second scenario, your decision is planned and deliberate. In each case, you feel regret, but you don't know how to deal with it. Do you try to ignore your feelings? How can you ignore your regret when you've violated your own values?

Sometimes we can conveniently "forget" smaller occurrences, but they may mount up. And the larger mistakes? The ones that have a deeper impact? What if you get caught up in a group mentality and damage someone's property, bully another person, or reveal someone else's intimate secret for your own gain? What if you seriously damage a friend's reputation? You know in these circumstances that you've made serious errors in judgment and action—and you may be having trouble not only forgiving yourself, but even living with yourself. Maybe you begin to have troubling feelings of shame or self-hatred.

In addition to dealing with your own difficult emotions, you'll have to cope with the pain you've caused others. What if you're facing the consequences, paying the price for your mistakes, and the person you've hurt can't forgive you? Will you be able to go on, forgive yourself, and start fresh? At times like these, you might find it difficult to differentiate between hating your actions and hating yourself.

Forgiving ourselves for our mistakes and our missteps can be difficult business. It's especially hard for a warrior who is trying to build a life based upon strong principles and noble ideals. Stumbling is all part of the journey. But sometimes, as we practice and practice these seven principles, we may falsely start to believe that we'll never falter. We forge ahead with strength and conviction—and then, when we do fail, we have a lot of trouble accepting that failure. Our own pride becomes our enemy.

Fortunately, you can move beyond these painful feelings. Peace will not come all at once. You'll need to draw upon the warrior's principles of perseverance and indomitable

## Room for Reflection

- How have other people hurt you? How have you hurt others? What do you understand about human beings because of these experiences and this pain?

- Have you ever held a grudge against someone? Were you able to get rid of these negative feelings? If so, how?

- What is a value of yours that you've ignored in the past—or that you think you might be tempted to abandon in a future time of weakness? What have you done to stay "on guard" against this happening?

- How do you forgive yourself and move forward when you feel especially self-critical?

spirit—and you'll also need to rely on love. Once you can look closely at yourself and admit that your *action* was wrong, but that *you* are still a person of worth, strength and potential, you can begin to love yourself again and to forgive yourself. Then you can also begin to see yourself as someone who is capable of having great love and sharing it with others.

As you work through the process of forgiving yourself, you may find that recommitting to your values is a good first step. Make a promise to yourself that you'll do better next time. Remind yourself of the ideals and values that you are striving to live by. Also remind yourself that even warriors make mistakes, sometimes big ones. Finally, continue working to show love and care for others through your daily actions. Do your best to reach out to other people with concern and kindness. The connections you make with others will help you stay positive, focused, and energized, and will remind you that the principle of love encompasses honestly loving other people *and* ourselves.

## A Story from the Warrior's Path

To a parent, love means caring for his or her child. Parents spend many hours working for their sons or daughters out of love. To a friend, love is looking out for one another and having each other's back. To either group, love means to sacrifice for the benefit of the other—to do things you might not always enjoy doing.

Love doesn't include doing a favor for a person just to get a reward or to be recognized. Love is to do a favor and expect nothing in return, to help someone when that person might not always return the favor. It is to do something out of the kindness of your heart and not for selfish purposes. No matter how disrespectful or different from you people might be, setting an example of love means showing courtesy and care to them anyway.

—Anthony, 14

## Closing Thoughts on Love

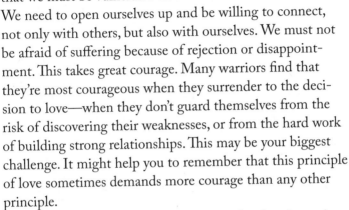

One of the amazing characteristics of love is that we must be vulnerable in order to love. We need to open ourselves up and be willing to connect, not only with others, but also with ourselves. We must not be afraid of suffering because of rejection or disappointment. This takes great courage. Many warriors find that they're most courageous when they surrender to the decision to love—when they don't guard themselves from the risk of discovering their weaknesses, or from the hard work of building strong relationships. This may be your biggest challenge. It might help you to remember that this principle of love sometimes demands more courage than any other principle.

Perhaps you've already begun to see that love is not just a feeling. It is a choice. And sometimes we have to make this choice in spite of negative feelings we have about other people or about ourselves. We must forge ahead despite pain and fear—and remind ourselves that warriors cannot truly be their best without the commitment to love others and themselves.

You'll probably find that one or two of the fundamentals in this chapter are especially difficult to practice. That's all right. Let some of the other warrior principles come into play when you feel like you're struggling. Maybe you'll persevere until you learn one of the fundamentals better. Or maybe you'll practice community service to help you understand more about the principle of love and how to make it part of your life.

As you take steps to build your warrior's heart, try to remember this: we do not truly love because of perfection. We love in spite of the imperfection in others and ourselves. And what a wonderful challenge that is! What imperfections do you recognize in yourself or in others—and how will you show love in spite of these imperfections?

# Afterword

Your journey through this book and your reflections about yourself and your life are the first steps you've taken to develop the heart of a warrior. You joined Master Yi and his young students as they studied the seven principles of courtesy, integrity, perseverance, self-control, indomitable spirit, community service, and love. You heard the words of your fellow warriors, describing the way they see these principles. Then you took further steps of your own as you practiced the fundamentals in each chapter along the way.

You may have felt frustrated at times on your journey. And you will likely feel frustrated at times in the future. When you face discouragement, stress, or sadness, remember that you are always growing. Bit by bit, day by day, you make progress toward your goals. And warriors focus on progress, not perfection.

The seven principles are ideals and guides—not measurements. They don't dictate the direction of your path or where your life will take you. But they can help you live your life with hope, enthusiasm, and joy, and they may inspire you to contribute to a more peaceful world.

Go now—with your warrior's heart—and live happily and peacefully!

# Using This Book with Students—A Guide for Teachers and Leaders

Whether you teach in the classroom, lead a youth group, coach a team, or work with teens in some other setting, *Heart of a Warrior* can help you guide young people as they learn about themselves, explore their ideas, and focus on their goals. *Heart of a Warrior* can be used in many different ways to inspire productive discussion, promote serious inquiry, and provide teens with useful strategies for living great lives. Try the following ideas with your group.

## Start with the Basics

Have a conversation about what it means to be a warrior. Use the following questions to get started.

- What are some qualities you believe a warrior possesses? Do you think the concept of a warrior presented in the book differs from what many people imagine when they think about warriors?
- List people from history who you see as true warriors. What do these people have in common with one another? How do they differ?
- Is there someone in your own life who you consider to be a modern warrior? How does this person demonstrate the heart of a warrior?

## Make Room for Reflection

Throughout *Heart of a Warrior*, "Room for Reflection" sections present prompts to spark discussion, writing, or reflection. Try the following ideas for using these questions with a group.

* Have each group member write down one of the "Room for Reflection" questions on a slip of paper and place it in a hat. Draw one question at a time and discuss as many as time allows.

* Ask each group member to choose any question from a "Room for Reflection" section and write a short personal response to it—a few honest words that she or he would not mind sharing. (There's no need to have students write their names on their responses.) Then collect the responses and redistribute them randomly. When students receive their fellow teens' personal responses, ask them each to "respond to the response" by asking another provocative question to encourage additional reflection and discussion. Discuss the questions and answers as a group.

* Set aside journaling time once a day, once a week, or however often suits your schedule. At the beginning of each journaling period, read a "Room for Reflection" question aloud (or ask a group member to do so) and invite teens to freewrite in response. Assure them that, even though the question may provide the initial spark for their journal entry, they can go in any direction they wish with their thoughts and writing.

## Put Your Heads Together

Hold a brainstorming session with your group based on an idea, story, or question from *Heart of a Warrior*. You could go in many different directions with this activity. For example, toss out ideas for additional fundamentals for each principle, or make a list of ways to put each principle into action today. Don't be afraid to get creative! The goal is simply to spark your group's imagination. You might brainstorm a list of animals, songs, or literary characters that teens associate with each principle. Or maybe, as a group, you could compose an acrostic poem for each principle. Just have fun and let the ideas fly.

## Introduce Master Yi

Consider and discuss Master Yi's words and messages.

- In the first chapter, Master Yi says, "The greatest learning often occurs after the teacher has left." Do you think this is true? Can you think of any examples of this in your own life?
- In every chapter, Master Yi says, "Looking is good. Seeing is better. Listening is good. Hearing is better." What does this mean to you?
- The teacher takes his student-warriors to a different place each day. What does each location have to do with the principle for that day?
- Invite a student (or students) to read one of Master Yi's poems aloud for the group. Then talk about what people think the poem means, what its imagery symbolizes, and how it makes them feel. Invite students to write their own poems about one of the seven principles.

## Act Out

If your group is large enough, divide it into small groups and assign a principle to each one. Have each group create and perform a short skit based on their assigned principle. Maybe they act out a scenario demonstrating the principle in action, or perhaps they role-play Master Yi talking with his students. Or, have each teen research a warrior from history and then assume the identity of that warrior to speak to the whole group about his or her life. If time allows, encourage positive discussion among the large group about what each performance portrayed.

## Look at the Big Picture

Invite students to take a broad view of the seven principles and talk about what they mean.

- If you could add another principle, what would it be?
- Why do you think Master Han added the last two principles of community service and love?
- Which principle means the most to you? Why?
- Think about the proverbs and sayings that open each chapter. How are they related to the principles? Which ones do you like best, and why?

## Create

Encourage students to express their creativity. Invite teens to work individually or in groups to create artistic representations of one of the principles or fundamentals: paint pictures, create collages, compose songs, write poems, or explore other mediums. If students have a hard time getting started, suggest that they write their own "Story from the Warrior's Path." When everyone has created a piece, hold a "gallery opening" of the work for friends, family, classmates, and other community members.

## Take It One Principle at a Time

In the rest of this guide, you'll find additional questions and exercises for each principle. These prompts are geared toward individual writing, private reflection, and self-exploration. However, many of these activities can easily be adapted for group discussion. You know your group best. Do what works for you.

In addition, you'll find suggestions for group projects that dovetail with each principle. These activities will help you take your group beyond your meeting space and out into the world to put the seven principles into action. Good wishes on your journey!

## The First Principle
# Courtesy

## Individual Exploration

- Take a few minutes to make a list of people who have helped you on your life journey so far. Then choose one person and write about how he or she helped you. Consider the situation you were in, how you felt before he or she helped you, what happened, and how you feel now.

- Think of someone you know who is very kind, and write about a situation in which you witnessed his or her kindness. Describe the physical features of the person, the setting, any words that were spoken, and the overall feeling you have when you remember the situation.

- Choose one of courtesy's four fundamentals and write about a time in your life when you displayed one of these traits. Remember that even the tiniest act can be important. Now think about a future situation where you might like to show more of this fundamental. Write about where and when you hope to show that quality.

## Group Projects

- Have your group make greeting cards that say courteous things, such as, "Have a great day!" or "Thanks for being you!" Hand them out at school or in the community, or mail them to friends and family—even if they live nearby.

- Work as "greeters" welcoming people to a local event or offer to be the hosts and guides for a school orientation program for new students or parents.

- One of the fundamentals of courtesy is "Show courtesy toward all—even your rivals." Ask your group to identify a current "rival" group (for example, an opposing athletic team or a rival school). Then invite your group to consider

ways to demonstrate courtesy toward this rival and choose
one or more of these ideas to carry out. Examples might
include painting a welcome banner for a visiting team or
writing a group letter expressing sportsmanlike encouragement to the rivals in an upcoming competition or
other endeavor.

## The Second Principle

# Integrity

## Individual Exploration

- In the middle of a sheet of paper, draw a circle and label it
  "ME." Then draw many lines extending outward from the
  circle. At the end of each line, write a term that character-
  izes you somehow (for example, dancer, family member,
  brown-eyed, kind, loyal friend, etc.). Reflect on one of
  these qualities, interests, or abilities. How important is
  it to who you are as a person? What experiences has it
  allowed you to have?

- Write down a few positive expressions that you'd like to
  remember. Ask friends and family for their suggestions
  and favorites, too. Then post these sayings and words in
  places where you'll see them every day—in your room, on
  a notebook, on the refrigerator, in your locker, etc. After a
  week or two, do you notice any differences in your outlook? Do you think that surrounding yourself with positive words helps you think and act more positively?

- Imagine someplace where you feel calm and peaceful.
  Write about that place, describing it in detail and explain-
  ing how it makes you feel. As you write, imagine yourself
  being there.

## Group Projects

* Ask group members to choose a piece of personal writing on integrity and contribute it to a compilation. Share these writings on a blog or submit them to be a weekly feature of a school or local paper. Encourage other people in the community to share their own views on integrity.

* Take your group to a meditation class to help them practice being still, invite a meditation teacher to address the group, or visit a park or other space and do the following exercise: Sit cross-legged on the ground or floor. Close your eyes and breathe slowly, being completely quiet. Get comfortable. Try to breathe rhythmically through your nose and imagine that each time you breathe out, your troubles leave you. Do this for 10 minutes or so. Afterward, invite group members to write or talk about how they feel.

* To spread the word about positive thought and positive action, have the group come up with an original slogan to inspire their school or community. As a group, work to get the slogan publicized within the community, and pledge to uphold that slogan through actions and words

## The Third Principle

# *Perseverance*

## Individual Exploration

* Focus on the present. Choose an object from your desk or book-bag and allow your senses to experience it. Feel its shape, look at it from many angles, smell it, listen as you tap it against a surface. Then write a few sentences about what you noticed.

- Make a list of hardships that you would find especially difficult to welcome. Choose one and write about how you'd feel if you faced this difficulty, how you might deal with it, and how it might affect you in the short and long term.

- Create a "Challenge List" for yourself of goals you'd like to achieve—even if you're not certain that you can. Your list may include goals for yourself at school, at home, or anywhere. The focus is not to try to do these things right away, but to think about things that you want to accomplish, and to seek inspiration to accept one of these challenges.

## Group Projects

- Ask each group member to research a true story about someone in history who showed perseverance. Then have each student write a brief monologue from the perspective of that person, telling his or her story. Create a short play from these monologues and perform it for friends, family, classmates, or others in the community.

- Hold a roundtable discussion in which teens name tasks they have difficulty undertaking or completing. Roundtable members can then offer suggestions for ways to approach and finish these tasks. As facilitator, encourage a broader discussion of what it means to persevere, how we can do so in the face of challenges, what the rewards of perseverance are, and similar topics.

- The fundamentals of perseverance are often reinforced through mental exercise and repetition. Invite the group to select and memorize an inspirational speech, story, or poem. Then, for an audience of family, friends, and other community members, have the group perform an oral interpretation of the entire piece, with each group member reciting a few lines from memory.

## The Fourth Principle
# Self-Control

## Individual Exploration

* Think about events in your life that seemed to be negative at the time, perhaps making you angry or afraid or disappointed. Choose one and write about what happened, how you reacted, and how you feel now. Do you still think of the experience as only a negative one? Or—now that time has passed—do you see some positive effects?

* Consider one of your personal goals, and estimate how long you think it might take you to reach it. Then come up with three detailed steps that you can take each day, every other day, or each week to make progress toward that goal. Write down these steps and make a point of following through on them. At the end of a month, assess your progress.

* Spend some time reflecting on your grade school days and the things you learned then, either in the classroom or outside of it. Focus on one "little thing" that you had to do over and over again. How well do you remember the task now? Did you enjoy doing it, or find it a chore? Was it a building block for something bigger? Do you see a benefit in it now that you didn't then?

## Group Projects

* Have the group create a "Responsibility Chart." Assign small tasks for each person to carry out daily or weekly for the benefit of the whole group, such as helping clean a classroom or recording meeting minutes. See if group members can carry out their responsibilities without being reminded.

- Encourage the group to come up with a "Take Charge and Improve" initiative within their school, organization, or community. Have group members identify an area that they believe needs improvement, declare their intent to "take charge," put together a detailed plan for addressing the need, and present their plan to the relevant administration. Encourage the group to accept responsibility for their plan's implementation.

- Have the group talk about the kinds of temptations young people sometimes have to say no to. Encourage discussion about why it's often difficult to say no, and brainstorm strategies for resisting temptation. Role-playing such scenarios can also be helpful.

## The Fifth Principle
# Indomitable Spirit

## Individual Exploration

- Reflect on a setback that you've experienced. Describe the situation and comment on your perspective now. What were your initial reactions to this setback? How did you deal with it? What do you think about it now that time has passed?

- You could think of enthusiasm as a "passion for" something. What is something you're passionate about? Describe the activity and your enthusiasm for it. Is it an artistic pursuit? Athletic? Emotional? Does it involve other people, or is it a solitary activity?

- Think about a time when you stepped forward. Write about the situation and how it made you feel. How about a time when you saw a chance to step forward, but didn't? Why didn't you? Do you wish you had? Why or why not?

## Group Projects

* Develop a plan for mentoring young people who need a boost. For example, your group could "adopt" a grade-school class, with each teen pairing up with a younger student and offering support, enthusiasm, and guidance in necessary (and ongoing) ways.

* Set up a weekend "spirit fair" at which teens can offer short informational sessions about activities or subjects that they are skilled in or passionate about. Invite people from school or the community to attend.

* Encourage group members to step forward for others by starting a "no bullying" campaign. Talk with the group about where and when they see bullying and teasing happening. Discuss what they should do about it, and how they can reach out to the people involved.

## The Sixth Principle
# Community Service

## Individual Exploration

* Compose a list of ideas for connecting with others in a positive way. How might you think beyond yourself and embrace the "Big I"?

* While we all have individual differences and personalities, all human beings are valuable and deserve respect. What are some factors that cause individuals or groups to be discriminated against? Have you ever been considered to have less worth than someone else? How did you feel? Or have you ever witnessed the mistreatment of another person because that person was different in some way? Write about your experience.

* Choose someone in your life you would truly like to listen to and get to know better. Write down some questions you could ask that would show your genuine interest. Be sincere when you write and ask your questions, and listen thoughtfully to the answers.

## Group Projects

* Spend a day helping out. Set up a visit for your group to a local food shelf, soup kitchen, animal shelter, or other organization that needs and welcomes volunteers.

* Have the group brainstorm a list of causes, charities, and service opportunities that they're interested in. Hold a vote to choose one, and then organize a fundraiser for that group.

* Approach the city council or civic group in your city, town, or neighborhood. Offer to be a "go-to group" for the community in times of need. Then embark on a publicized project and invite other youth groups from the community to join you. You might even create special shirts for your "go-to" team.

## The Seventh Principle

# Love

## Individual Exploration

* At what times do you feel isolated from others—lonely, cut off, separated? Recall one particular time and write about it. What caused your isolation? How did you feel, and how did you address and eventually resolve this situation?

* Write about someone you know who doesn't seem to judge others very often. How does this person interact with others? How do people respond to him or her?

• Forgiving others can be very difficult. In your experience, why is this fundamental so hard to embrace? Write about someone you've had trouble forgiving. How did that person hurt you? Were you eventually able to forgive him or her? If so, how did you feel afterward? If not, what do you think has to happen for forgiveness to occur?

## Group Projects

• Have group members find adages or sayings about love and share these with the group, along with some comments about why they like the message. Compile these sayings in a booklet—perhaps illustrated with photographs and art by group members—and (with the necessary permission) distribute it at school, home, or in the community.

• Visit a local eldercare facility and have students talk with, read to, play cards with, or just spend time with residents.

• Organize a reading for friends, family, or the public at which students may each bring and read an original or a published poem that celebrates the human capacity to care for and love others or to improve our world.

# Index

# Acknowledgments

This book has come about because of the influence of countless people, human beings who have enriched my life beyond my understanding. Although he passed on in 1996, Master Cha Kyo Han, founder of the Universal Taekwondo Federation, maintains his influence to this day—not only in my life but also in the lives of students throughout the world. He is a huge inspiration for this book. I would never have come under the tutelage of Master Han had it not been for Dr. Jin Wook Choi, my Korean brother and very first teacher, who introduced me to the martial arts in 1967, in the backyard of my parents' home. Little did I know that our relationship would bring about the blessings I have enjoyed from thousands of students in the high school classroom, on the college campus, and in the Taekwondo dojang. I can never thank Dr. Choi enough for his advice and help with this book—and for his long and powerful influence in my life.

Instrumental in my personal growth and in the progress of many, many students is certainly Master Paul Irvin, copresident of the Universal Taekwondo Federation, who personifies what it means to be a master in the martial arts. He, along with international instructor Bruce Helman, a true expert and great teacher, offered their encouragement with this project and their constructive criticism in an early draft. In addition, I express my gratitude to Master Eddie Truman, who offered his wide expertise to my students, helped open my mind, and remains my friend.

As a long-time educator in Community Unit School District 200 of Illinois, I benefited from professional and personal relationships with wise and caring administrators, teachers, and staff. I must thank them for their energy and their daily inspiration for me and thousands of students. Naturally, no teacher can exist without pupils. And so I owe a great debt to all of my students, since 1973, in every environment. They have taught me lessons I have tried to internalize and pass along. I am certainly grateful to those who provided their voices and stories throughout this book.

The Board of Directors and the supporters of Pathways for Achievement deserve special gratitude for the vision and the guidance they have provided for teenagers since 1996. They represent the capacity of the human heart. Instrumental in the Pathways efforts are Christopher Grodoski and Lee Prior, martial artists and middle school teachers, who offered their thoughts on the book. I also thank my relatives and friends, including my nephew Tom Langlas, for their criticism, encouragement, and expertise, enabling me to undertake the final stages of the project.

In addition, my wife Michelle, my son Jack, and my daughter Chelsea have encouraged me in my teaching, maintained stability in our home when I have been instructing students or studying, and motivated me through the days and years of our lives together. They have enriched the meaning of love and family and have personified the seven warrior principles throughout their lives.

Of course, I remain indebted to the entire team at Free Spirit Publishing. The creative and dedicated professionals there—especially my editor, Alison Behnke—have never wavered in their faith or their commitment. Working with them has been a joy and an inspiration. I also express my thanks to Austin Schlenker and Claire Hauge, two teen readers who provided their thoughtful and timely perspectives on *Heart of a Warrior*.

# About the Author

Jim Langlas is an educator, a Taekwondo master, and a writer. Born in Waterloo, Iowa, in 1951, he began studying Taekwondo in his middle teens under the guidance of Jin Wook Choi. In 1973, Jim came under the guidance of Master Cha Kyo Han, who remained his teacher until Master Han's death in 1996. In 1974, Jim was a member of the U.S. Taekwondo Team and won a gold medal at the International Taekwondo Federation World Championships in Montreal. In 1980, he opened his own Taekwondo dojang.

Jim received his B.A. in English and physical education from the University of St. Thomas, his Master of Arts in teaching English from Northwestern University, and his Ph.D. in English from Northern Illinois University. He taught English, instructed Taekwondo, and coached in Wheaton-Warrenville Community Unit School District in Illinois for 33 years, where he also served as English Department Chair. In 1996, he founded Pathways for Achievement, an organization devoted to helping teenagers in Chicago's suburbs succeed in school and life. In 2003 he founded and chaired Community Partners in Poetry to foster an interest in poetry among all ages. He received the Studs Terkel Humanities Service Award from the State of Illinois in 2005. His poetry has appeared in many journals, among them *Poetry* and *American Scholar*. Jim presently serves as the Universal Taekwondo Federation's copresident and teaches English at Edison State College. He and his wife, Michelle, live in Naples, Florida.

# Other Great Books from Free Spirit

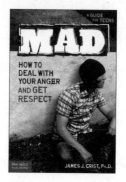

**What Do You Really Want?**
How to Set a Goal and Go for It!
A Guide for Teens
*by Beverly K. Bachel*
For ages 11 & up.
*144 pp.; softcover; illust.; 6" x 9"*

**Mad**
How to Deal with Your Anger
and Get Respect
*by James J. Crist, Ph.D.*
For ages 13 & up.
*160 pp.; softcover; 2-color; illust.; 6" x 9"*

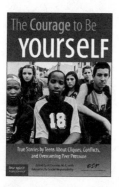

**The Courage to Be Yourself**
True Stories by Teens About Cliques,
Conflicts, and Overcoming Peer Pressure
*edited by Al Desetta, M.A., with
Educators for Social Responsibility*
For ages 13 & up.
*160 pp.; softcover; 6" x 9"*

**Fighting Invisible Tigers**
Stress Management for Teens
(Revised & Updated Third Edition)
*by Earl Hipp*
For ages 11 & up.
*144 pp.; softcover; 2-color; illust.; 6" x 9"*

*For pricing information, to place an order, or to request a free catalog, contact:*
**Free Spirit Publishing Inc.**
**217 Fifth Avenue North • Suite 200 • Minneapolis, MN 55401-1299**
**toll-free 800.735.7323 • local 612.338.2068**
**fax 612.337.5050 • help4kids@freespirit.com• www.freespirit.com**